Recent Research in Psychology

Robert W. Proctor Daniel J. Weeks

The Goal of B.F. Skinner and Behavior Analysis

Springer-Verlag
New York Berlin Heidelberg
London Paris Tokyo Hong Kong

Robert W. Proctor
Department of Psychological Sciences
Purdue University
West Lafayette, Indiana 47907
USA

Daniel J. Weeks
Motor Behavior Lab
School of Physical Education
Lakehead University
Thunder Bay, Ontario P7B 5E1
Canada

Library of Congress Cataloging-in-Publication Data
Proctor, Robert W.
The goal of B.F. Skinner and behavior analysis / Robert W. Proctor, Daniel J. Weeks.
p. cm. — (Recent research in psychology)
Includes bibliographical references.
ISBN 0-387-97236-6 (alk. paper)
1. Behaviorism (Psychology) 2. Skinner, B.F. (Burrhus Frederic), 1904– . 3. Psychology, Experimental. I. Weeks, Daniel J. II. Title. III. Series.
BF199.P76 1990
150.19′434—dc20 89-77961

Printed on acid-free paper.

Camera-ready copy provided by the authors.
Printed and bound by Edwards Brothers, Ann Arbor, Michigan.
Printed in the United States of America.

9 8 7 6 5 4 3 2 1

ISBN 0-387-97236-6 Springer-Verlag New York Berlin Heidelberg
ISBN 3-540-97236-6 Springer-Verlag Berlin Heidelberg New York

One way of contrasting science and dogma is to say that a scientist accepts facts as given and belief systems as tentative, whereas a dogmatist accepts the belief systems as given - facts are irrelevant

McCain and Segal
(1982, p. 43)

FOREWORD

It has been suggested by some that the Skinnerian system appears to be less theoretical than it really is, because alternatives are infrequently examined or even granted recognition. It also has been suggested that this allows shaky ideas to enjoy more credibility than perhaps may be deserved. Still others have suggested that the Skinnerian system is more than just another psychological theory: it is a world view. None can doubt that important and, to some individuals, very disturbing societal and scientific consequences follow from the ideas of B. F. Skinner. Given this scenario, it should come as no surprise to radical behaviorists that some have classified them as dogmatists possessed of ideas inimical to scientific and political freedom in the bargain.

Must radical behaviorism be dogmatic? I have been able to escape that impression reading, as I do, the *Journal of the Experimental Analysis of Behavior*. Who is to say that the matching law, for example, has been subjected to less rigorous scientific examination than other hypotheses in psychology? The authors of this book largely agree with this general assessment.

If radical behaviorism can be free of dogmatism, what then is the fuss? The authors contend that the world view that accompanies radical behaviorism leads to dogmatism more frequently than other viewpoints. Is that the case? The authors, in the spirit of science, present their general argument in the form of a series of hypotheses. They attempt to support each hypothesis with evidence. The authors have carefully examined many sources, ranging from the writings of radical behaviorists to various critics of that viewpoint. They approached their task with considerable seriousness of purpose, and regardless of whether the reader is in accord with the conclusions that are reached, these conclusions are worthy of serious consideration. Of course, the quality of the exercise cannot be judged on the basis of the authors' intentions. Rather, it depends on the quality of the arguments and the supporting evidence. It could not be otherwise. As scholars, the authors would not wish it to be otherwise. Nor should we.

Were I a radical behaviorist, my inclination would be to examine the arguments and evidence presented here point by point. I would reply by addressing the picture that emerges from these points, if that can be done. I hope that one or more radical behaviorists will approach this book in exactly that spirit. It is not up to me to prejudge the results of such an exercise. Nevertheless, I earnestly hope it will occur, and I strongly suspect that the authors of this book hope so too.

E. J. Capaldi
Purdue University

PREFACE

The work of B. F. Skinner on reinforcement principles forms the core of a subdivision of psychology, which is referred to as *the experimental analysis of behavior*. Members of this subdivision, termed behavior analysts, have extended Skinner's system to provide a complete interpretation of human action. Through Skinner's public prominence, the impact of his writings has been much greater outside of psychology than within. Also, Skinner and other behavior analysts assert that the Skinnerian approach to the study of human behavior is technologically superior to other approaches. Moreover, many behavior analysts charge that the field of psychology unjustly fails to acknowledge behavior analysis as the superior approach.

Our intention in this book is to examine the evidence for the self-asserted superiority of the behavior-analytic approach and to assess the validity of the claims made by those who adhere to it. Our interest in evaluating the experimental analysis of behavior arises from our previous association with an eclectic psychology department that was changed to one with a behavior-analytic emphasis. During the period of change, we witnessed a number of events in which the behavior-analytic views of psychology and of science were imposed dogmatically and constructive discussion of opposing views suppressed. The resident behavior analysts displayed a general intolerance toward other approaches in psychology and characterized those approaches as scientifically inferior. Yet, despite the behavior analysts' self-described scientific superiority, they seemed to engage in relatively little scientific research.

The question that led us initially into this project was to what extent the activities that we observed in our particular situation were characteristic of the behavior-analytic subdivision as a whole. A cursory examination of the behavior-analytic literature revealed that the activities that we observed first-hand did seem to be representative. Thus, through a more detailed examination, we approached this project with the goal of understanding the behavior-analytic conceptions of science and psychology, and why these conceptions differ so dramatically from those generally acknowledged in contemporary psychology. We realize that no single index would reflect the views of all behavior analysts, but we have made every attempt to present what we consider to be the prototypical views.

The philosophy of radical behaviorism, as articulated by B. F. Skinner, serves as the source of most behavior-analytic views. This philosophy provides a "world view" in which all aspects of the behavior of organisms are determined entirely by environmental contingencies. This view is inconsistent with a number of assumptions held by most approaches within contemporary psychology. Because the philosophy of radical behaviorism provides a world view, all other views are superceded and intolerance of other approaches is promoted. The world view dictates the questions, the methods, and the form that answers must take -- in short, the conceptions of science and psychology. Yet, an important feature of science in general is that competing views and approaches are considered in the resolution of issues. Thus, eclecticism and tolerance are virtues in science that seem to be necessary assets in the pursuit of truth.

As we shall argue, intolerance is manifest in the experimental analysis of behavior and has led to a clear demarcation between behavior analysis and contemporary psychology. We shall show that many behavior analysts dogmatically oppose the types of questions regarding human behavior that are deemed relevant in contemporary psychology, the methods by which behavioral data are collected in attempting to answer these questions, and the causal explanations that are considered acceptable. As a consequence, behavior analysts tend to regard competing approaches within contemporary psychology as obstacles rather than as viable alternatives that deserve scientific respect and evaluation. Yet, from a scientific perspective, competing approaches should not be viewed as obstacles and treated with intolerance, but rather "as if" they possess truth value. The validity of such truth value then can be evaluated on the basis of empirical evidence.

By accepting a world view that is based on the philosophy of radical behaviorism, the role of truth value is minimized. As a consequence, the virtues that the scientific method offers in pursuit of truth value -- e.g., "as if" consideration of competing approaches, ecclecticism, and tolerance -- become impediments. Our point in this book is not that radical behaviorism is undeserving of being evaluated relative to other approaches, but that no competing scientific approach should serve as the basis of a world view. Because the various approaches are constantly in flux, the only legitimate point of departure in pursuit of the truth is a view of the world that is dictated by a rational philosophy of science.

As experimental psychologists, we approached this project as we would in investigating any other behavioral phenomena. As such, the level of assessment that we employed was to evaluate the field of behavior analysis "as if" it had truth value. This evaluation was conducted in three phases, which correspond to the three major parts of the book.

The first part presents an introduction to B. F. Skinner and the field of the experimental analysis of behavior. Part I also examines the state of contemporary psychology by considering three alternative approaches that Skinner has characterized as providing unjust obstacles to behavior analysis. Thus, Part I formulates the important questions and issues pertaining to the activities of the field of behavior analysis. Part II examines the relation of behavior analysis to the larger enterprises of psychology, science, and pseudoscience. These examinations provide evidence regarding activities of behavior analysts that bear on the questions and issues developed in Part I. In Part III, we provide a causal explanation of the evidence. The implications of our explanation for the experimental analysis of behavior and for the discipline of psychology then are explored.

The general theme of our explanation is that the inability of the experimental analysis of behavior to become the predominant approach in psychology is a function of misplaced goals in the practice of science. This goal structure has contributed to a relative lack of research activity and empirical evidence to support many of the behavior-analytic claims, particularly those regarding human behavior. In place of empirical evidence, behavior analysts often have relied on interpretive analyses of human behavior that are a function of the presuppositions and philosophical underpinnings of the Skinnerian system. Because psychology strives to be a scientific discipline, empirical evidence is the primary determinant by which views are accepted. Thus, the lack of hard evidence for the behavior-analytic interpretations precludes behavior analysis from receiving more serious consideration from the field of scientific psychology.

Although we have many personal anecdotes that pertain to the issues that are addressed in this book, these anecdotes are not included. Rather, our explanation is based on documented evidence. Thus, we would hope that, as is the case with any scientific explanation, it will be evaluated and judged on the basis of the strength of the evidence.

We would like to thank the following individuals for their support of this project. First, we are indebted to Dr. Robert F. Kidd, the series editor at

Springer-Verlag, for understanding the value of considering the issues that we discuss. Second, we appreciate the interactions that we had with our former colleagues which helped us to understand the "big picture". These colleagues include Lanie Dornier, Sam Green, Allen Hess, Rupert Nacoste, and Gil Reeve, among others. Third, the project has benefited greatly from the constant challenges to our arguments provided by Janet Proctor. Fourth, we thank Julie Smith for typing the manuscript and Trish Van Zandt for helping with the graphics. Finally, we would like to thank our new colleague, E. J. Capaldi, for his encouragement and invaluable judgment on the key issues.

RWP

DJW

West Lafayette

1989

CONTENTS

PART I

WHAT IS THE EXPERIMENTAL ANALYSIS OF BEHAVIOR AND WHY HAS IT NOT BECOME PSYCHOLOGY?

1

THE EXPERIMENTAL ANALYSIS OF BEHAVIOR

The emergence of psychology as an independent, scientific discipline usually is dated to the opening of Wilhelm Wundt's lab at Leipzig, Germany, in 1879. In the ensuing 110 years, the discipline has become a multi-faceted science that encompasses most aspects of human behavior. However, people outside of psychology typically are unaware of the substantial progress that has been made. Of the handful of psychologists who have reached public prominence, Burrhus Frederic Skinner is the individual who is identified most often as the representative of scientific psychology. For example, Guttman (1977) notes that a 1975 survey showed Skinner to be the best known scientist in the United States, at that time.

1.1 B. F. SKINNER

B. F. Skinner was born in 1904 in Susquehana, Pennsylvania. He majored in English at Hamilton College, graduating in 1926. After graduation, Skinner spent two years attempting to establish a career as a writer. He then entered the graduate program in psychology at Harvard University, receiving his Ph.D. in 1931. Skinner remained at Harvard in a postdoctoral position for five years, after which time he took a faculty position at the University of Minnesota. He left Minnesota in 1945 to assume the chair of the Department of Psychology at Indiana University. In 1948, Skinner returned to Harvard, where he has remained since. He currently is the Edgar Pierce Professor of Psychology Emeritus at Harvard. Skinner's awards and distinctions include the Distinguished Scientific Contribution Award of the American Psychological Association; the National Medal of Science, awarded by Lyndon B. Johnson; and the Gold Medal Award of the American Psychological Foundation.

Skinner's first book was *The Behavior of Organisms*, published in 1938. Other books include *Science and Human Behavior* (1953), *Verbal Behavior* (1957), and *Contingencies of*

Reinforcement (1969). Skinner's fame outside of psychology stems in part from his popularized books, such as *Walden Two* (Skinner, 1948) and *Beyond Freedom and Dignity* (Skinner, 1971), that have been targeted for the lay public. In these writings, a case is made for the extension of Skinner's views regarding human behavior to a variety of societal concerns, thereby culminating in a Utopian society.

Skinner's academic career has focused on the investigation of operant conditioning, which refers to changes in an organism's behavior that occur as a function of responses being reinforced (positively or negatively) or punished. Analogous to evolutionary theory, reinforcement contingencies imposed by the environment are assumed to select certain responses over others in various contexts. Skinner's work on reinforcement contingencies (e.g., Skinner, 1938) forms the core of a relatively small subdivision of psychology, which is known as *the experimental analysis of behavior* (TEAB).

Consistent with the evolutionary analogy, TEAB often is referred to by its adherents as the natural science of behavior. Advocates of the Skinnerian tradition, who typically call themselves *behavior analysts*, believe that the basic tenets of reinforcement theory provide a unified account of all human behavior (e.g., Harzem & Williams, 1983). Moreover, behavior analysts believe that examinations of interactions between environmental variables and behavior provide the keys to solving the problems that confront psychology and society (e.g., Harzem, 1987; Pennypacker, 1986; Skinner, 1971).

Although B. F. Skinner's views are prominent in the media and in academia, they are not representative of the majority of psychologists. For example, Epstein (1984) indicates that behavior analysts make up less than 3% of the membership of the American Psychological Association. Because the modal views of Skinner and other behavior analysts deviate in many ways from those of mainstream psychologists, the views can be characterized as being "particularly extreme" (Schwartz, 1978, p. 7). Despite this fact, the views of Skinner, along with those of Sigmund Freud, collectively serve to define the field of psychology in the public's mind, a problem that Stanovich (1989) refers to as "the Skinner-Freud problem".

Thus, paradoxically, although Skinner and the field of TEAB admittedly have had relatively minimal influence within scientific psychology (e.g., Skinner, 1987), their views nevertheless have come to be regarded by many people outside of that science as representative of the discipline. Both behavior analysts and non-behavior analysts have recognized this paradox and questioned why the disparity of impact has arisen (e.g., Guttman, 1977; Skinner, 1987; Stanovich, 1989). The present book examines the paradox and provides a resolution through considering the goals and values of TEAB.

1.2 THE EXPERIMENTAL ANALYSIS OF BEHAVIOR

Two basic types of associative learning traditionally have been distinguished in psychology (Bower & Hilgard, 1981). One type is *classical conditioning*, which refers to learning that involves the co-occurrence of environmental events. The other type is referred to as *instrumental conditioning*. The distinguishing feature of the latter type of learning is that the organism's own behavior is crucial in producing an environmental consequence.

The early work on classical conditioning typically is credited to Ivan P. Pavlov (1849-1936), although this work was preceded by the related research of I. M. Sechenov.

Classical conditioning involves the establishment of reflexive responses to stimuli that previously did not elicit the responses. For example, Pavlov found that an unconditioned, reflexive salivary response by a dog to meat powder could be conditioned to occur when a sound was presented. Conditioning took place when the sound occurred immediately before presentation of the meat powder. After regular pairing in this manner, the sound stimulus came to elicit the salivary response.

The strongest advocate of classical conditioning as the basis for human behavior was John B. Watson (1878-1958), who is regarded as responsible for the adoption of a behavioristic orientation by psychology early in the twentieth century. Watson argued that all human behavior could be explained by classical conditioning. Among his contributions was the demonstration that emotional responses could be classically conditioned. Watson showed that when a loud noise, which produced a fear response for a child, was paired with the child's reaching for a white rat, the fear response came to be elicited by the rat alone (Watson & Rayner, 1920). Watson asserted that conditioned emotional reactions of this type comprise the majority of human emotions.

The early work on instrumental conditioning was performed by Edward L. Thorndike (1874-1949). This work documented the role of behavioral consequences in learning. Through his experimental investigations of felines trying to escape puzzle boxes, Thorndike proposed *the law of effect*: The effect of a response on the environment determines whether a stimulus-response connection will be formed and, in turn, whether a behavior is likely to recur under similar circumstances in the future.

Skinner followed Thorndike's lead in placing emphasis on instrumental conditioning, which is re-termed *operant conditioning* in Skinner's system. In Skinner's terminology, an operant is an identifiable unit of behavior for which no correlated stimulus can be detected. Critical to the notion of operant conditioning is the concept of a *reinforcer*. Reinforcers are any consequential events that modify the likelihood that the operant behavior will occur again. The contingent relation between the operant response and the reinforcer is called the *two-term contingency* (Lee, 1988).

In operant conditioning, the behavior is not controlled directly by an eliciting stimulus. But environmental stimuli that precede the response are important in another way. Such stimuli are referred to as *discriminative stimuli*. These stimuli serve as cues to indicate when particular behaviors will be reinforced and, thus, "set the occasion upon which a response will be reinforced, and therefore...upon which it will occur" (Skinner, 1938, p. 22). Thus, the inclusion of discriminative stimuli completes the *three-term contingency*, which is the cornerstone of the Skinnerian system (Sidman, 1960).

The approach of TEAB is characterized best by methodological directives provided by Skinner (Fantino & Logan, 1979): (1) Accounts should rely exclusively on directly-observable phenomena; (2) psychology should be an independent science of behavior that invokes neither subjective mental events nor speculative physiological mechanisms; and (3) the basic datum should be rate of responding, presented in the form of a cumulative record as a function of time. In other words, an experimental analysis of behavior should describe the environmental conditions under which specific behaviors occur and account for these behaviors only in terms of past environmental conditions.

To study operant conditioning, Skinner designed an apparatus that has become known widely as the "Skinner box". This apparatus is a soundproof box in which a rat can depress a lever or a pigeon can peck a key to receive a food pellet or some other reinforcer. The lever or key is connected to a recorder that plots a cumulative record of the number of responses as a function of time that the animal is in the box. One contribution of Skinner and TEAB has been to specify various schedules for the delivery of reinforcement (e.g., Ferster & Skinner, 1957).

Reinforcement of any given response may occur according to time between responses or response frequency. Under *continuous reinforcement*, every response is reinforced. When reinforcement subsequently is discontinued, *extinction* is said to occur. A *reinforcement schedule*, then, refers to the delivery of reinforcement along a continuum from continuous reinforcement to extinction. *Ratio schedules* require that a specified number of responses be emitted prior to a response being reinforced. In other words, the schedule defines a ratio of total responses to reinforced responses. Alternatively, *interval schedules* require that a specified amount of time elapse prior to a response being reinforced.

These two basic schedule types can be

broken down further into fixed and variable classes. *Fixed schedules* require that a constant number of responses or a constant elapsed time occur between reinforcements. Conversely, *variable schedules* require only an average number of responses or elapsed time occur between reinforcements. A factorial combination of these distinctions yields four basic schedule types: fixed ratio, fixed interval, variable ratio, and variable interval. Responding under each of these basic schedules has a characteristic topography. Moreover, the basic schedules can be permuted to form complex variations (Reynolds, 1975).

One critical aspect of the Skinnerian system is that, through the reinforcement contingencies, the environment functions to control behavior. Given the emphasis on environmental control, most behavior-analytic research has been conducted in the laboratory with non-human species, particularly rats and pigeons. With this subject population, behavior analysts have been able to discover a number of additional behavioral principles (e.g., stimulus equivalence; Sidman, Cresson, & Willson-Morris, 1974). Moreover, they have been successful in gaining control over relatively complex behaviors in these lower organisms (e.g., Project Pigeon; Skinner,

1960).

The behavior-management techniques that emerged from the laboratory research of behavior analysts have been adopted by professionals in mental health, educational, and correctional settings, among others. The further development of these techniques has been conducted under the banner of *applied behavior analysis*. The behavior-analytic procedures have proved to be a useful means for behavioral management in these special environments. However, despite the widespread use and apparent success of the behavior-management techniques in applied settings, basic research in the experimental analysis of human behavior has a relatively short history (Buskist, 1983; Harzem & Williams, 1983; H. L. Miller, 1983). Thus, a somewhat curious imbalance exists in which the application of behavior-analytic techniques to human populations far outweighs the empirical validation from tightly controlled, basic research with humans.

1.3 A WORLD VIEW

If it were the case that Skinner and other behavior analysts were trying only to demonstrate that they had a viable means for providing insight into certain aspects of behavior, we would not take much issue with their views. Indeed, as a practical means of managing human behavior in tightly controlled environments, the potential usefulness of the behavior-analytic techniques has yet to be fully realized (e.g., Dickinson, 1976). However, it is clear that Skinner and behavior analysts have a much broader agenda (e.g., Pennypacker, 1986). That is, they propose a world view in which the principles of Skinnerian behaviorism provide a complete account of all human behavior.

In the opinion of two behavior analysts, "Radical behaviorism's commitment to developing a truly thorough-going world view has been one of its most definitive features" (Malagodi & Jackson, 1989, p. 31). Moreover, according to the editor of *The Behavior Analyst*, "The fact is that behavior analysts see themselves as having a world view that is incompatible with most of psychology" (S. S. Glenn, personal communication, June 21, 1989). A consequence of this world view is that other approaches within psychology that are inconsistent with the dictates of TEAB are regarded as illegitimate (see Lee, 1988; Malagodi & Jackson, 1989). Because of the assumed completeness of the account provided by TEAB (e.g., Harzem & Williams, 1983), behavior analysts propose that their methods and techniques should form the basis of a technology used to control human societies.

Thus, behavior analysts have little doubt that their system is *the* correct system for predicting and controlling behavior. Moreover, Skinner's views have had considerable impact outside of scientific psychology. Yet, paradoxically, the Skinnerian system is not widely accepted within psychology. In Skinner's (1987) words:

> For more than half a century the experimental analysis of behavior as a function of environmental variables and the use of that analysis in the interpretation and modification of behavior in the world at large have reached into every field of traditional psychology. Yet they have not *become* psychology, and the question is, Why not? (p. 782)

We turn to this question in the succeeding chapters.

2

THE THREE OBSTACLES

In answer to his question of why TEAB has not *become* psychology, Skinner (1987) asserts, "Perhaps answers can be found in looking at three formidable obstacles that have stood in the path of an experimental analysis of behavior" (p. 782). The obstacles to which Skinner refers are humanistic psychology, psychotherapy, and cognitive psychology. Through examining why Skinner perceives these alternative viewpoints as posing obstacles to the development of TEAB, further insight into the nature of TEAB is gained.

2.1 HUMANISTIC PSYCHOLOGY

According to Skinner (1987), "Humanistic

psychologists have attacked behavioral science...like creationists in their attack on secular humanists" (p. 783). These attacks are attributed by him to threats regarding personal freedom and "dehumanization" that humanistic psychologists perceive in the behavior-analytic movement. Skinner asserts that, in retaliation, humanistic psychologists "often challenge the content or selection of textbooks, the appointment of teachers and administrators, the design of curricula, and the allocation of funds" (p. 783). Yet, these strong assertions are made with no supporting documentation.

Examination of the historical record indicates that humanistic psychology hardly can be regarded as a serious impediment to the development of TEAB as a viable science of psychology. The behavior-analytic approach has been advocated for approximately 50 years, since the publication of *The Behavior of Organisms* (Skinner, 1938). The first conference devoted to the experimental analysis of behavior was held in 1947 (Hineline & Laties, 1987). In contrast, prior to 1958, humanistic psychology had no appreciable existence as a distinct approach (Shaffer, 1978). The year 1958 marks the publication of the book, *Humanistic Psychology*, by John Cohen. Similarly, whereas the Society for the Experimental Analysis of Behavior was founded in 1957, the American Association for Humanistic Psychology was not formed until 1962 and did not hold its first international conference until 1970.

The American Psychological Association recognized behavior analysis as a distinct subdiscipline (Division 25) in 1965, but did not bestow similar recognition to humanistic psychology (Division 32) until 1970. Also, the primary journal for basic behavior analysis, the *Journal of the Experimental Analysis of Behavior*, began publication in 1958, while the inaugural issue of *Humanistic Psychology* did not appear until 1961. In short, the historical record indicates that the chronological development of TEAB as a distinct subdiscipline was relatively contemporaneous with that of humanistic psychology, with the formal establishment of TEAB actually preceding that of humanistic psychology.

Not only did the establishment of TEAB precede that of humanistic psychology, but the atmosphere within academic psychology was more in accord with a behavioral approach. That is, around the time that TEAB was being established, behaviorism in general already was ingrained as the predominant philosophical position within psychology (Baars, 1986). As a consequence, psychologists were disposed toward accepting behavioristic, rather than nonbehavioristic, approaches. Thus, the behavior-analytic approach, through its relation to behaviorism, should have posed an obstacle to the development of humanistic psychology, rather than vice versa. It is perhaps remarkable, then, that "within the short span of a decade, humanistic psychology had become recognized as a distinct school or approach, with a philosophy, a research method, and an array of applications that were uniquely its own" (Shaffer, 1978, p. 3).

One contributing factor to the rapid growth of humanistic psychology was the emergence of a new "collective conscience" in society. Humanistic psychology was proposed at a point in which there was increasing concern with what it means to be human. That is, the collective societal attitude was that interpersonal relationships, feelings, emotions, and other basic psychological needs had been too neglected in the culture. Humanistic psychology provided a means for re-integrating these basic needs back into a complete view of humans.

The basic premise of humanistic psychology is that humans are innately good and growth-oriented (Royce & Mos, 1981; Shaffer, 1978). The approach is characterized by an emphasis on subjective phenomenology. That is, it places considerable importance on a person's immediate experience in determining reality. Further, humanistic psychology views human beings as having freedom of choice and autonomy. This freedom occurs within the restrictions that are determined by the environment. The broad emphasis is on a holistic view, in which humans are regarded as possessing an essential integrity (Rogers, 1981). There is no attempt to reduce a person's experiences into more basic drives.

When the American Association of Humanistic Psychology was founded, the "Articles of Association" characterized the field in the following manner:

> Humanistic psychology is primarily an orientation toward the whole of psychology rather than a distinct area or school. It stands for the respect for the worth of persons, respect for differences of approach, open-mindedness as to acceptable methods, and interest in exploration of new aspects of human behavior. As a "third force" in contemporary psychology, it is

> concerned with topics having little place in existing theories and systems: e.g., love, creativity, self, growth, organism, basic need-gratification, self-actualization, higher values, being, becoming, spontaneity, play, humor, affection, naturalness, warmth, ego-transcendence, objectivity, autonomy, responsibility, meaning, fair play, transcendental experience, peak experience, courage, and related concepts. (p. 2)

Even from this brief overview of humanistic psychology, it should be apparent that the approach developed in part as a reaction to behaviorism. Humanistic psychologists held that behaviorism was less concerned than it should be with many of the central aspects of the human experience. But, nevertheless, they remained committed to many of the central features of behaviorism. Specifically, while humanistic psychologists assume that it is essential to regard humans as having freedom, they acknowledge that an assumption of determinism is a necessary precursor to the scientific study of cause-effect relations.

Despite the emphasis that humanistic psychologists place on the internal dynamics of being human, overt behavior is not excluded from consideration (Krippner et al., 1988). But neither is the human experience simply reduced to a collection of behaviors, as is the case in a more radical view of behaviorism. Thus, although humanistic psychology arose, at least in part, as a reaction to perceived weaknesses in the behavioristic orientation, it nevertheless assimilated many of the crucial aspects of that system into its own.

Despite the bold efforts of humanistic psychologists to develop a broader view of humankind that retains at least loose connections with a behavioristic orientation, Skinner (1987) dismisses these efforts as reflecting nothing more than the "antiscience stance of humanistic psychology" (p. 784). In response to Skinner's characterization of humanistic psychology as "antiscience", several humanistic psychologists have expressed outrage at Skinner's misrepresentation of the field (Krippner et al., 1988). According to them, "Skinner has presented an egregiously inaccurate characterization of humanistic psychology that ill becomes one of his stature" (p. 819).

Despite Skinner's assertion to the contrary, Krippner et al. (1988) note that they and other humanistic psychologists "are firmly committed to the scientific enterprise" (p. 819). Students trained in humanistic psychology receive courses in a variety of research methods and in all of the major schools of psychological thought. Thus, humanistic psychology has sought to maintain ties with the science of psychology by at least remaining consistent with its basic tenets. As we will show later, behavior analysis can make no such similar claim.

The humanistic movement never was opposed to the scientific study of human behavior (Shaffer, 1978). It simply was concerned with whether questions asked from the perspective of behaviorism alone could provide a complete picture of human nature. To meet that concern, humanistic psychologists have attempted to understand the "glue" that puts the collection of human behaviors into a meaningful whole. In doing so, they have rejected a "hard" science approach to theorizing but have attempted to confirm many of their speculations through empirical evidence. Whereas Skinner could question whether the subject matter of humanistic psychology will yield a meaningful science of human behavior, his assertion that humanistic psychologists take an antiscience stance simply is not borne out by the evidence.

In summary, the evidence indicates that humanistic psychology could not have posed an unjust obstacle to the development of TEAB. First, behavior analysis and humanistic psychology show time-courses to their early development that favor the primacy of behavior analysis. Second, psychology was predisposed to a behavioristic position rather than to a humanistic position. Third, humanistic psychology remained committed to the importance of the scientific approach. And fourth, the intent of humanistic psychologists was to augment rather than displace the scientific study of human behavior. As one consequence, many of the activities of humanistic psychologists have gone on outside of mainstream scientific psychology.

That humanistic psychology was intended to complement the scientific study of human behavior is captured in the following quotation from *The Psychology of Science*, by A. H. Maslow. Maslow, one of the foremost proponents of the humanistic tradition, writes:

> I conceive this to be not a divisive effort to oppose one "wrong" view with another "right" view, nor to cast out anything. The conception of science in general and of psychology in general, of which this book is a sample, is *inclusive* of mechanistic science. I believe mechanistic science (which in psychology takes the form of behaviorism) to be not incorrect but rather too narrow and limited to serve as a *general* or comprehensive philosophy. (1966, p. 5)

2.2 PSYCHOTHERAPY

According to Skinner (1987), "certain exigencies of the helping professions are another obstacle in the path of a scientific analysis of behavior" (p. 783). He argues that the practice of psychotherapy has blocked the progress of behavior analysis. By Skinner's assessment, the primary reason why psychotherapy creates an obstacle is that "psychotherapists must talk with their clients and, with rare exceptions, do so in everyday English, which is heavy laden with references to internal causes" (p. 783). In Skinner's view, one consequence of appealing to internal causes in therapy is that such causes are incorporated inappropriately into theoretical explanations. For example, he notes that psychoanalysts "construct theories in terms of memories, feelings, and states of mind" (p. 783). Skinner goes on to argue that although references to internal causes may be of some practical value in therapy, they have no genuine explanatory value in psychological theory.

Skinner does not specify those approaches that he would group under the term psychotherapy, so we must assume that he intended the term to be defined broadly. As such, at least six categories of psychotherapy can be distinguished (Patterson, 1986): cognitive approaches; learning theory approaches; psychoanalytic approaches; perceptual-phenomenological approaches; existential psychotherapy; and eclectic psychotherapy. It should be noted that the scope of the approaches that comprise psychotherapy is quite diverse. Moreover, the trend in recent years has been toward eclecticism (Hess, 1981; Patterson, 1986).

Terms taken from the language of the layman do play a role in many, but not all, of the theoretical frameworks developed for psychotherapy. The question then becomes one of whether the use of this language has impeded the development of these theoretical positions. This question is important, because theory provides the foundation for the scientific practice of psychotherapy (Brammer & Shostrum, 1977). Indeed, the premise of the widely accepted scientist-practitioner model is that the therapist should be trained broadly as a scientist (Bickman, 1987). But what does it mean for a therapist to be trained as a scientist?

According to Brammer and Shostrum (1977), two related meanings should be distinguished. The first sense is that the therapist is a skilled observer of the therapeutic process, capable of describing accurately the observed behavior. The second sense is that the scientific "attitude" is employed by the therapist to evaluate the inferences made about the observations. It is in this second, more important sense that the practitioner is a scientist in his/her approach to therapy.

One way in which the scientific attitude is realized in the work of therapists is captured by the following scenario (Brammer & Shostrum, 1977). The therapist starts with a problem, then observes the product of the client-therapist interaction and formulates hypotheses about the interaction. These hypotheses are in the form of inferences that are based on the direct observations. Once the therapist has refined a set of hypotheses, a plausible theory can be deduced. This theory then is used to predict further events in therapy, with predictions tested against actual events. The goal is to bring the predictions and observations in closer agreement. To the extent that this goal is met, an increased understanding of the behavioral problem is developed.

The primary point is that psychotherapists have maintained application of a scientific attitude both in their evaluations of the merits of scientific research and in the practice of psychotherapy. Thus, to accuse psychotherapy of being an impediment to the development of behavior analysis solely on the basis of the language used in its theory building simply is not acceptable. Because of psychotherapists' allegiance to the scientific method through a scientific attitude, an acceptable attack on the legitimacy of psychotherapy would have to be grounded in scientific evidence. That is, if scientists of other persuasions, cognitive, behavior analytic, or otherwise, wish to charge that the legitimacy of psychotherapy has been hindered by allowing lay language to infiltrate the basic theory, they must provide empirical evidence to support the charge. Although behavior-analytic writings are replete with "in principle" arguments, which are similarly unacceptable (Machan, 1974), Skinner (1987) and other behavior analysts have been remiss in providing arguments that are grounded in empirical evidence.

Skinner's (1987) assertion that psychotherapy poses an obstacle to TEAB seems to reflect a broader charge. For example, Harzem (1987) dismisses community psychology as "oriented to immediate remedy rather than 'serious academic psychology'" (p. 177) and characterizes the rise of clinical psychology as resulting in a deferral of the experimental analysis of human behavior. Likewise, Hopkins (1987) notes that "Keller and Schoenfeld (1950) and Skinner (1953) had only speculated about the applicability of the principles [of reinforcement theory] to important human behaviors, but their speculations were much more rational than the collection of inconsistent mentalistic speculations that I had learned from clinical psychology" (p. 340). Thus, the charges raised against psychotherapy seem to reflect more than just a concern with the use of lay language.

Unfortunately, it is true that not all of the psychotherapeutic trends that have gained popularity have been grounded in a sound, scientific basis (Corsini, 1981). A number of "quick fix" therapies, such as primal scream and nude encounter groups, have occurred. However, as scientifically-oriented clinicians clarified the therapeutic elements of psychotherapy, these fads waned quickly when the evidence indicated that they would be of little long-term value (Garfield & Bergin, 1986).

In sum, the therapies that have endured are those that are related most closely to the established body of empirical knowledge. Consequently, "pop" psychological therapies have posed at most minor obstacles to the development of more sound psychotherapeutic procedures. Thus, it is difficult to believe that these trends could have posed major impediments to the development of behavior analysis.

2.3 COGNITIVE PSYCHOLOGY

The third obstacle proposed by Skinner (1987), that of cognitive psychology, requires more serious consideration, because it currently is the predominant approach taken in scientific psychology. As noted by M. W. Eysenck (1984), "over the past 20 years or so, experimental psychology has become increasingly synonymous with cognitive psychology" (p. xiii). As a consequence, and in contrast to TEAB, no distinct division for cognitive psychology exists within the American Psychological Association.

As with humanistic psychology, the historical record indicates that the formal development of TEAB as a subdiscipline of psychology preceded that of cognitive psychology. Whereas TEAB has been established for approximately 50 years, the "cognitive revolution" has occurred only over the past 25 years (Baars, 1986; Hilgard, 1987). The formalization of cognitive psychology usually is tied to the publication of Ulric Neisser's book, *Cognitive Psychology*, in 1967. The journal with the same name began publication in 1968, a decade after the appearance of the *Journal of the Experimental Analysis of Behavior*. Thus, again, from a chronological standpoint, cognitive psychology could not have posed an obstacle during the formative years of TEAB.

The rise of cognitive psychology was due in part to a relative lack of progress within the more restricted approaches that preceded it (Baars, 1986). Further, its emergence as the predominant paradigm for psychology was predicated by major advances in communications engineering, computer science, linguistics, neuroscience, quantitative modeling, and other fields (Lachman, Lachman, & Butterfield, 1979). These advances provided a common theoretical language for making precise, testable explanations of human behavior, in terminology that is consistent with that used in the analysis of inanimate systems (Posner, 1986). Moreover, the rise of cognitive psychology as the pre-eminent force in scientific psychology neither was impeded nor enhanced significantly by humanistic psychology or psychotherapy. Rather, numerous experimental results, theoretical analyses, and technological advances dictated the shift to cognitive explanations of many behavioral phenomena.

Behavior analysts typically attribute the current wide acceptance of cognitive psychology to a variety of social pressures, rather than to sound, scientific reasons. For example, Fraley and Vargas (1986) state that "psychology as a discipline reflects strongly the surrounding culture and what the marketplace wants," thus producing psychologists "who speak with the language of a philosophy of science in which intentions and feelings rule, not unlike the longstanding lay 'common sense' position, but now hyped as cognitive science" (pp. 48 and 49). Such characterizations fail to acknowledge the historical reality that behaviorism, as a distinct school, reigned in American psychology for approximately 50 years (Hilgard, 1987). Moreover, the cognitive revolution occurred because the aforementioned advances in psychology and related disciplines converged to indicate that cognitive explanations were both appropriate and necessary to explain many aspects of behavior (Baars, 1986; Lachman et al., 1979).

The obstacle posed today by cognitive psychology to TEAB is scientifically valid, in that the cognitive approach has met with considerable success in explaining complex human behavior. Thus, for any competing approach to be given serious consideration, it must account for a broad range of human behavior in a manner that is consistent with accepted scientific criteria. For the approach to become the predominant paradigm, it must be demonstrated to be scientifically superior. Skinner and other behavior analysts have made strong claims regarding the superiority of the behavior-analytic framework for understanding human behavior, yet the scientific evidence supporting this presumed superiority is meager, even according to many behavior analysts (see Buskist, 1983; Harzem & Williams, 1983; Kunkel, 1987; H. L. Miller, 1983).

2.4 SUMMARY

Careful evaluation indicates that none of the three "obstacles" seem to account for why TEAB has failed to become the pre-eminent force within psychology that Skinner envisioned. Although humanistic psychology and psychotherapy are not "hard" sciences, in the sense that they do not have the primary commitment of advancing basic knowledge regarding human behavior, they are committed to a judicious application of that knowledge. To this end, both have recognized the need for adopting a scientific attitude when applying and evaluating therapeutic principles and their empirical basis.

This scientific attitude precludes humanistic psychology and psychotherapy from being impediments to the development of behavior analysis as a legitimate science of human behavior. That is, being armed with the scientific attitude and trained as scientist/practitioners, professional psychologists are in a unique position to evaluate the scientific merits and therapeutic implications of any psychological theory. Therefore, given the requisite evidence, behavior-analytic principles and techniques would receive fair and appropriate consideration. Such evidence has been provided only for special populations, and for these populations, the application of behavior-analytic principles is widespread.

In contrast, cognitive psychology does pose a serious obstacle to TEAB, but only in a competitive, scientific sense. The sheer weight of the evidence indicates that cognitive psychology provides a fruitful approach for developing a useful, scientific knowledge-base regarding human behavior. Thus any competing approach, behavior analytic or otherwise, that seeks pre-eminent status in the behavioral sciences must confront the obstacle posed by this evidence. Such a requirement is not an unfair criterion placed on behavior analysis, but a sound application of the scientific method.

3

CONTEMPORARY SCIENTIFIC PSYCHOLOGY

The previous chapter showed that humanistic psychology, psychotherapy, and cognitive psychology have not posed unfair obstacles to the development of TEAB. That Skinner chose to look to these "obstacles" for answers to the question of why TEAB has not *become* psychology seems attributable to two incorrect assumptions that he made regarding the nature and status of contemporary psychology. These assumptions are that (a) contemporary psychology is not the science of behavior and (b) psychology is not regarded as a member of the scientific community. In the present chapter, we present evidence inconsistent with Skinner's assumptions and then propose an alternative hypothesis for why TEAB has not become psychology.

3.1 PSYCHOLOGY AS THE SCIENCE OF BEHAVIOR

Chapter 1 ended with a statement by Skinner (1987) that questioned why "*the* experimental analysis of behavior" (p. 782, emphasis ours) has not become psychology. But his answer, given at the beginning of Chapter 2, describes obstacles that have stood in the path of "*an* experimental analysis of behavior" (p. 782, emphasis ours). This subtle shift from the definite article "the" to the indefinite article "an" conveys the crucial implication that if obstacles have blocked the development of *TEAB*, then they also have blocked the emergence of *any* experimental analysis of behavior. Skinner likely intended this implication, given that the question originated in an article entitled, "Whatever happened to psychology as the science of behavior?"

Characterizing behavior analysis as *the* experimental analysis of behavior necessarily precludes that scientific knowledge regarding behavior could have been advanced by any other perspective. Yet, the specific version of behavioral analysis advocated by Skinner and his followers is but one of many possible analyses (Amsel, 1989; Blackman, 1974). In fact, the primary concern of all approaches within contemporary, scientific psychology is the explanation, prediction, and control of behavior (see, e.g., Kerlinger, 1973). Although TEAB has not become psychology, the discipline of scientific psychology has experienced revolution and unprecedented growth during the past 50 years. This period of growth has seen the emergence of a number of experimental analyses of behavior, with the information-processing approach being most influential for much of experimental psychology in recent years.

Skinner (1987) regards most of the developments within scientific psychology as being inconsistent with his view that psychology should be the science of behavior. For example, he notes that most introductory textbooks refer to psychology as the "science of behavior *and* mental life" (p. 784), which he considers to be self-contradictory. Similarily, when lamenting the advent of information processing, Skinner indicates that "it was no longer necessary to construct settings in which to observe behavior, one could simply describe them. Rather than observe what people actually did, one could simply ask them what they would probably do" (p. 784).

Yet, the most important ingredient in the rise of cognitive psychology and information processing was the establishment of objective methods that enabled relatively precise inferences about the nature of processing to be made from behavioral measures (Bower, 1975). These inferences have proved to be useful means for predicting the behavior of humans (e.g., Kahneman, Slovic, & Tversky, 1983) and nonhumans (e.g., Capaldi & Miller, 1988) alike. Thus, the foundation of contemporary, scientific psychology is systematic, controlled observations of behavior.

Skinner (1987) also asserts in a sarcastic tone that the information-processing approach made troublesome problems "vanish like magic. A detailed study of sensation and perception was no longer needed, one could simply speak of processing information" (p. 784). But, the very nature of the information-processing approach requires a detailed analysis and understanding of the computational theory, how that theory can be implemented by representations and processes, and how such representations and processes can be realized physically (Marr, 1982). In short, rather than making troublesome problems vanish by definition, as Skinner implies, the information-processing approach introduced a whole new level of precision that enabled researchers to address the problems more effectively (see, e.g., Posner, 1986).

3.2 PSYCHOLOGY AND THE SCIENTIFIC COMMUNITY

In his second assumption, Skinner (1987) alleges that psychology is not regarded as a member of the scientific community and attempts to answer the question of, "Why not?" He declares that "unable to offer a useful conception of its subject matter, psychology has not formed good relations with the other sciences" (p. 785). As evidence, he observes that "for more than two years *Science* has not published a single article on psychology" (p. 784).

Science has not ceased to publish psychology articles, as Skinner implies, but publications of psychology in *Science* have in fact decreased. However, the journal's editor, Daniel E. Koshland, has stressed that the decline is "not a basic prejudice" (Hostetler, 1988, p.4) but is attributable to two factors: (a) fewer manuscripts are being submitted and (b) a larger percentage of the submitted manuscripts are being rejected *by psychologists*. According to William Dember, the American Psychological Association's representative to the governing body that publishes *Science* (the American Association for the Advancement of Science), the latter of these factors is due to the fact that psychologists "are harsher in their criticisms and standards" (p. 4). Thus, the small number of psychology articles submitted to and published in *Science* is attributable largely to the rigor that is self-imposed by psychologists, rather than to a lack of respect for psychological research by the American Association for the Advancement of Science. Moreover, psychology is well-represented in other broad scientific publications, such as the *American Scientist* and *Scientific American*.

The best example of the scientific credibility accorded contemporary psychology is the key role that it plays in the emerging interdisciplinary field of cognitive science (Norman, 1981). In this field, psychologists work together with computer scientists, neuroscientists, engineers, anthropologists, sociologists, linguists, philosophers, and others. Epstein (1984) notes that in a recent report commissioned by the White House and the National Science Foundation, cognitive science "was placed on equal footing with *mathematics, the atmospheric sciences, astronomy and astrophysics, agricultural research, neuroscience, human health effects of hazardous chemical exposure, materials science, chemistry, immunology, solid earth science, and computer science*" (p. 111). Although Epstein, a former student of Skinner's, regards cognitive science as an unfortunate alliance that "will leave its mark on psychology for many years" (p. 112), it is clear from the equal footing that cognitive science is given with the other sciences that contemporary psychology is highly regarded.

In addition to cognitive science, psychology plays a key role in many emerging inter-disciplinary fields, such as human-factors engineering, neuroscience, and movement science, among others. Within these fields, contemporary psychology provides crucial information regarding the factors that influence behavior. Thus, in contrast to Skinner's assumption that psychology is not scientifically respectable, the evidence indicates that the respect accorded psychology by the other sciences is greater than ever before.

3.3 THE STATUS OF CONTEMPORARY PSYCHOLOGY

Skinner's (1987) assertion that psychology is not an accepted science reflects his view that psychology has accomplished little and needs to be "rescued" if it is to make contributions in the future (Skinner, 1983). This view is echoed by other behavior analysts (e.g., Harzem, 1987; Lee, 1988, Liegland, 1984). For example, Lee argues that psychology has not been able to provide a useful body of data and summarizes the critical literature as depicting a discipline that is "replete with confusion, malaise, doubt, disillusionment, and mutual antagonism, and which lacks enthusiasm, commitment and direction" (p. 1). However, the prosperity of the discipline argues to the contrary. During the century since psychology was established as an independent discipline, it has amassed an impressive knowledge base (see, e.g., Hilgard, 1987). Moreover, the progressive accumulation of knowledge within psychology has enabled an ever-increasing application of this knowledge to a variety of problems (e.g., Berger, Pezdek, & Banks, 1987).

A good example involves the areas of human perception and performance. Scientific research in these areas predates the formalization of psychology as a separate discipline (e.g., Donders, 1868/1969; Fechner, 1860/1966). Moreover, current research methods and knowledge relate to this early work but extend well beyond it (Posner, 1982). The extensive research that has occurred in recent years has culminated in a two volume handbook that summarizes the basic knowledge (Boff, Kaufman, & Thomas, 1986) and a three volume engineering data compendium that provides this knowledge in a form useful for systems design (Boff & Lincoln, 1988). Additionally, engineering models have been developed from the basic research findings that enable quantitative predictions for human performance in a variety of settings (e.g., Card, Moran, & Newell, 1986). Similar advances in basic and applied knowledge are apparent in virtually all of the sub-disciplines of scientific psychology.

Thus, by the criteria of basic knowledge, productivity, and application, scientific psychology is flourishing. In the face of this evidence, it is difficult to see how Skinner and other behavior analysts can maintain such pessimistic views of psychology. But, as we will show in the next section, maintaining views such as these seems to be an inevitable consequence of operating within the behavior-analytic system.

3.4 AN ALTERNATIVE HYPOTHESIS: THE GOAL OF TEAB

In seeking to answer his question of why TEAB has not become psychology, Skinner suggested that humanistic psychology, psychotherapy, and cognitive psychology have posed unjust obstacles to TEAB's ascension. Yet, as we already have documented, the evidence indicates that aside from providing legitimate competing scientific conceptions, the alternative approaches within psychology have not posed obstacles. Similarly, the evidence questions the assumptions that led Skinner to implicate the three obstacles. Contrary to those assumptions, psychology as the study of behavior is alive and well among the other sciences (Stanovich, 1989). Thus, Skinner's assumptions, as well as his conclusions, are at variance with the evidence. Nevertheless, the question remains as to why TEAB has not become psychology.

Rather than appealing to conditions of the academic environment, as Skinner did, we propose an alternative hypothesis that attributes the failings of TEAB to its internal activities. We propose that the critical factor that has deterred TEAB from a more prominent role in psychology is the fundamental assumption that TEAB is *the* science of behavior. We hypothesize that it is this assumption, and the conviction with which behavior analysts adhere to it as the focus of their world view, that drives their activities. Consequently, the largest proportion of these activities is directed toward the basic goal of the adoption and survival of TEAB. This survival goal serves to organize the behavior-analytic agenda and structure the behavior that accompanies pursuit of that goal.

That survival constitutes the primary goal of TEAB is demonstrated in several ways. These include a stated behavior-analytic national agenda for increasing the number of behavior analysts on university faculty and influencing public policy (Johnston & Shook, 1987), a reluctance to engage in activities that are not consistent with their philosophical commitments (e.g., Lee, 1989, Malagodi & Jackson, 1989), and a desire to make TEAB "the dominant intellectual force of the 21st century" (Pennypacker, 1986, p. 148).

It is not surprising that within the behavior-analytic culture, adoption and survival constitute the central goal to which activities are directed. In Skinner's words, "Survival is the only value according to which a culture is eventually to be judged, and any practice that furthers survival has survival value by definition" (1971, p. 130). Thus, by Skinner's assessment, cultural practices and activities are to be judged according to their survival value.

Consequently, to maximize the likelihood of attaining the survival goal, survival value becomes the criterion for determining the activities to which efforts should be directed.

The goal of the adoption and survival of behavior analysis is stated explicitly in many writings and implicitly in many others. For example, in a special issue of the *Journal of the Experimental Analysis of Behavior* devoted to the future of TEAB, the editors emphasize that they oppose "developments that, if pervasive, would entail a loss of identity for behavior analysis through a merging with older more conventional, views in psychology" (Lattal & Harzem, 1984, p. 349). As well, Fraley and Vargas (1986) proclaim that "the study of behavior differs fundamentally from the study of the psyche and logically cannot share the same discipline" (p. 47). In reference to the discipline of behavior analysis, Morris (1985) asserts, "If a scientific community [TEAB] does not arrange for contingencies *that assure its survival*, then so much the worse for that community" (p. 108, emphasis ours). Similarly, Pennypacker (1986) bemoans, "Highly effective technologies flowing from the discipline of behavior analysis have not been widely adopted, thus threatening the survival of the discipline itself" (p. 147).

Consistent with these statements, Pennypacker (1986) and others often refer to TEAB, rather than psychology, as "the discipline". In fact, training programs propose that students be trained "in conceptual and experimental analysis of behavior, the application of behavior principles, and the administration of behavioral programs" (Chase & Wylie, 1985, p. 159), but not psychology. Even when some exposure to psychology is advocated, the exposure is in the context of encouraging dismissal of these other alternatives (EAHB Programs, 1983).

Our hypothesized relation between the survival goal of TEAB and the activities of behavior analysts provides a context in which to make sense of Skinner's (1987) characterizations of contemporary psychology. Because Skinner and behavior analysts hold as a central assumption that TEAB is *the* science of behavior, it would make little sense to look internally for answers. Thus, Skinner was forced to implicate the three predominant approaches in contemporary psychology as obstacles, because no credibility can be afforded to any alternative view.

These external obstacles had to be

characterized as "unjust", because they have blocked the ascendancy of *the* legitimate view. Consequently, if there can be no legitimate science of behavior other than TEAB, Skinner had no option but to deride contemporary psychology as being non-behavioral and non-scientific. In sum, Skinner's claims regarding contemporary psychology follow directly from the assumption that TEAB is *the* science of behavior and from the accompanying goal of survival for that science.

Contemporary psychology places considerable emphasis on the importance of goal-directedness in accounting for human action (e.g., Anderson, 1983; G. A. Miller, Galanter, & Pribram, 1960). Therefore, examining the actions of behavior analysts in relation to the survival goal should provide insight into their behavior. If, as we contend, the primary goal of behavior analysts is not the acquisition of scientific knowledge, as it is in contemporary psychology, then many of the behavior-analytic practices will be at variance with those of contemporary psychology. We pursue this issue in the following section by considering the relation of TEAB to psychology, science, and pseudoscience.

PART II

RELATION OF THE EXPERIMENTAL ANALYSIS OF BEHAVIOR TO PSYCHOLOGY, SCIENCE, AND PSEUDOSCIENCE

4

RELATION TO PSYCHOLOGY

If one facet of the primary goal of TEAB is to ensure its survival as a distinct discipline, then open participation in the science of psychology would be precluded. That is, participation in scientific psychology would place the survival of TEAB as a distinct discipline at jeopardy by allowing it to be evaluated relative to other approaches. Such ongoing evaluation could result in the assimilation of some behavior-analytic views into scientific psychology and the rejection of others. Thus, if behavior analysts do not have the goal of just contributing to scientific psychology but of survival of their discipline, commonalities with the parent discipline that might serve as the basis for assimilation should be kept to a minimum.

In the present chapter, we show that the positions advocated by behavior analysts contrast in several ways with those that are predominant in contemporary, scientific psychology. These distinctions in prescribed methods and subject matter are sufficiently great so as to preclude much interaction between TEAB and contemporary, scientific psychology.

4.1 DISTINCTION BETWEEN TEAB AND EXPERIMENTAL PSYCHOLOGY

The label, "the experimental analysis of behavior," contains several terms that are used widely in psychology, but often with different meanings. As a consequence, the potential exists for incorrect inferences to be made about TEAB and its relation to psychology.

As implied by the term "experimental," TEAB often employs experimental methods. However, TEAB is not synonymous with experimental psychology. Very little of the basic research of behavior analysts appears in the four sections of the *Journal of Experimental*

Psychology, which is the primary research journal of the American Psychological Association, or in any other journals that would be regarded as major outlets for psychological research.

As implied by the term "analysis", TEAB involves analysis of behavioral data. This analysis requires "identifying the component parts or relations that comprise a complex whole" (Johnston & Pennypacker, 1980, p. 24), which is consistent with the basic tenets of experimental psychology. However, whereas experimental psychology stresses quantitative verification of observed relations and mathematical rigor, TEAB focuses primarily on descriptive presentation of the observed behavior. For example, Skinner (1983a) states that he became concerned when the psychology department at Harvard "began to drift toward mathematical psychology" (p. 224). As part of his concern, Skinner submitted a memorandum in which he commented, "To me, it is a gesture of voluntary bankruptcy to turn to mathematicians for the next advances in psychology" (p. 224).

As implied by the term "behavior", TEAB is a form of behaviorism. However, as noted previously, it is not the only form. Rather, there are many other varieties of behaviorism that operate under very different premises.

In fact, most contemporary psychology is behavioral, in the sense of basing theories on observable behavior (Baars, 1986). The form of behaviorism preferred by many behavior analysts is *radical behaviorism*. This form of behaviorism stresses that behavior is determined by environmental contingencies and denies the existence of subjective entities (e.g., Skinner, 1979).

A consequence of the above three points is that the use of the definite article "the", rather than the indefinite article "an", to refer to TEAB is misleading. That is, because the type of analysis provided by TEAB is only one of several possible experimental analyses of behavior, the TEAB sub-discipline is called more appropriately "an" experimental analysis of behavior (Blackman, 1974).

4.2 ISOLATION OF SKINNER

Skinner's career has been characterized from the start by being isolated to a considerable degree from the field of psychology.

According to Skinner (1982), the only formal training in psychology that he received as an undergraduate lasted 10 minutes. As a consequence, he entered graduate school as a "newcomer to the field of psychology [who] initially knew comparatively little about the discipline" (Coleman, 1985, p. 90). However, Skinner had read works of a few authors (e.g., H. G. Wells and Bertrand Russell) that "converted him to behaviorism even before he had taken any courses in psychology" (Baars, 1986, p. 62). Thus, according to Catania and Harnad (1988), Skinner "had become a committed behaviorist by the time he entered Harvard University as a graduate student" (p. 489).

Despite receiving his Ph.D. in psychology, Skinner (1979) emphasizes that he received little formal training in the discipline. He indicates that in preparation for his comprehensive examinations, "I had only completed two courses in psychology, neither of them covering much ground" (p. 34). Moreover, he adds, "Nor was I ever to learn much more psychology at Harvard....I never learned how to read the 'literature' in psychology, and the literature remained largely unread by me" (p. 34). However, rather than regarding Skinner's isolation as a deficiency, behavior analysts tend to view it positively. For example, Fraley and Vargas (1986) conclude that "remaining in such an isolated position facilitated developing his strong conviction that behavior was a subject matter to be analyzed in its own right" (p. 53). But Skinner's rudimentary knowledge of psychology ensured that his work would be relatively isolated from that of the rest of psychology.

Following graduate school, Skinner's prominence arose as a result of works that had their primary influence outside of psychology. Skinner gained his credentials through his impact on applied areas, such as the field of education. Moreover, Skinner's philosophy of radical behaviorism has been more widely accepted in those applied areas than within established psychology (Guttman, 1977).

4.3 ISOLATION OF BEHAVIOR ANALYSIS

The experimental analysis of behavior has been isolated from psychology, to at least some extent, since its inception.

Skinner's relative isolation from the discipline of psychology served as a model for behavior analysts (see e.g., Krantz, 1971), with the isolation being formalized with the founding of the *Journal of the Experimental Analysis of Behavior* in 1958.

One consequence of the founding of the journal was to ensure that the views of behavior analysts would have only minimal influence on the field of psychology in the ensuing years, because their research would be published primarily outside of mainstream psychology.

During the past 30 years, this self-chosen isolation of behavior analysts has persisted, becoming even more extreme. During that period, several additional journals devoted to the behavior-analytic perspective have been initiated (e.g., the *Journal of Applied Behavior Analysis*, *The Behavior Analyst*), and relatively little work by behavior analysts has been published in psychology journals (see, e.g., Krantz, 1971; Lee, 1988). Because the behavior-analytic journals form the core knowledge-base for TEAB, and because they have little interrelation with other psychology journals, the knowledge and terminology of behavior analysts is largely orthogonal to that of contemporary psychology.

An initial attempt to formalize the isolation through program curricula was made by Keller and Schoenfeld (1949). While at Columbia, they undertook a restructuring of the Introductory Psychology course and then extended this restructuring to encompass the entire undergraduate program. The restructuring was built around Skinner's (1938) book, *The Behavior of Organisms*, such that virtually all of the topics within psychology were presented from the behavior-analytic perspective. The apparent logic behind the restriction of the educational program to behavior-analytic views was articulated by Keller in a 1945 letter to Skinner, in which he related the circumstances regarding the restructuring. According to Keller, "Beginners get the point if you don't let 'em read the junk that is now marketed as psychology" (Skinner, 1979, p. 307).

The implications of such a drastic restructuring of curricula did not go unnoticed. Concerned by the potential implications, Wendt (1949) charged:

> The requirement by a department of adherence to any system of thought in its courses, be it Wundtian structuralism, neo-Thomistic humanism, or Skinnerism, eventually results in an inbred department and in its isolation from the rest of the science and from other disciplines. (p. 426)

Wendt continued by depicting the likely scenario that would accompany adoption of such a restrictive program. This scenario culminates in the adoption of "cult-like" behavior of those involved.

Keller and Schoenfeld (1949) reported that their program changes were well-received by the students and proposed that it serve as a model for educational practices. However, Wendt (1949) questioned whether the enthusiasm of the students was attributable to the core material or to the mechanics of the program. In his words:

> I recognize that the Columbia system is enthusiastically received by the students. But all cults have that advantage which rests on the fact, well-known to students of propaganda, that simplification introduced into confusion has high acceptance value. The worth of an educational policy must rather be evaluated by its long-run contributions to the pursuit of truth. To that end our old tradition of reasonable academic freedom and intentional diversification of staff seems better adapted. Systems have their

> function when eagerly developed by individuals, but their administrative imposition on a college can be only harmful in the end. (p. 426)

The trend toward the isolation of TEAB from psychology through formal curricula for the training of behavior analysts continues today. In recent years, recommendations advocate only minimal exposure to the basic areas of psychology (e.g., Chase & Wylie, 1985; Fraley & Vargas, 1986; Morris, 1985). Indeed, some behavior analysts stress the importance of keeping students and faculty even from being exposed to non-behavior-analytic views (e.g., Fraley & Vargas, 1986) and of innoculating students to make their "verbal repertoires more resistant to change" (Morse & Bruns, 1983) if exposure occurs. Thus, the training models for behavior analysis not only prevent students from acquiring the basic knowledge necessary for them to relate TEAB to the rest of psychology, but actively discourage them from trying to do so.

Interactions between behavior analysts and non-behavior-analytic colleagues are discouraged because, in the words of Fraley and Vargas (1986), "no amount or kind of graduate training prevents the drift toward mentalism in a faculty member subjected to the continuous audience control of a cognitive community" (p. 51). Similarly, in acknowledging that "behavior analysts have shown little interest in developing cooperative -- even cordial -- relations with psychologists of other persuasions," Linda Hayes, the editor of *Behavior Analysis* (the official publication of Division 25 of the American Psychological Association), states, "Fruitful interchanges between behavior analysts and other psychologists can be expected only when the underlying philosophical systems of those psychologies are compatible with that of behavior analysis" (1988, p. 2). Hayes concludes that "fruitful interchange seems more likely with other disciplines" (p. 2).

The culmination of this isolationist tendency is that many behavior analysts hold that their subject matter and needs are sufficiently unique to warrant severing all ties with psychology and establishing TEAB as a separate field (e.g., Epstein, 1984, 1985; Fraley & Vargas, 1986). That behavior analysts should encourage a formal separation of TEAB from the psychological study of human behavior is hardly surprising, given that Skinner admits that he was largely incognizant of the psychological literature when he formulated the basic tenets of TEAB.

4.4 ON INFERENCES ABOUT MENTAL EVENTS

Much, but not all, of experimental psychology accepts a view that is referred to as cognitive psychology. The major difference between the approaches taken by cognitive psychologists and by behavior analysts is that the former allow for inferences to be made about underlying mental representations and processes in order to understand behavior, whereas the latter opt for explanations solely in terms of behaviors and their consequences.

The rise of cognitive psychology to its preeminent position often is referred to as the *cognitive revolution* (Baars, 1986; Hilgard, 1987). As is the case with most contemporary psychology, theories in cognitive psychology are based primarily on behavioral data. However, the data often are interpreted in terms of the "information-processing" framework, in which the basic assumption is that a sequence of mental events occurs between a stimulus and an overt response.

Behavior analysts tend to use misleading

examples of cognitive explanations that imply that such explanations, at best, are extraneous (Wasserman, 1983). For example, Blackman (1974) indicates that the phenomenon of conditioned suppression (i.e., disruption of instrumental responding following an aversive stimulus, such as shock) could be interpreted in the following cognitive terms: "One might suggest that the rat *knows* that he is about to *experience* a shock which he will not *like*" (p. 218). However, such caricatures miss the point that cognitive explanations are neither proposed nor accepted capriciously. Rather, the explanations are linked to objective, experimental data, and several findings must converge to support a particular explanation before it is given much credence (Garner, Hake, & Eriksen, 1956).

The point that many behavior analysts seem to miss is that cognitive constructs are used only when their inclusion enables more accurate prediction. Moreover, the nature of the proposed construct is, whenever possible, kept consistent with what is known about the physiology of the organism (Fodor, 1983). Even in the trite example provided by Blackman (1974), attributing knowledge to the rat is justified if inclusion of the concept allows for greater predictability of future behavior. As an example, recent research by Capaldi and his colleagues (e.g., Capaldi & Miller, 1988) has shown that predicting the behavior of rats in a straight-alley runway is enhanced significantly by allowing for the possibility that the rats can count the lag between reinforced trials. Endowing the rat with a cognitive architecture that enables counting was done only when it was dictated by the data.

4.5 ON RESEARCH METHODS

A major difference between mainstream experimental psychologists and behavior analysts is that the former adhere to a flexible rule governing the selection of psychological research designs. A specific research design is selected according to the particular problem or situation that is being investigated.

Books on research methods customarily present a wide variety of methods, including observational techniques, correlational designs, between- and within-subject group experimental designs, and single-subject designs (e.g., Kantowitz, Roediger, & Elmes, 1988; Kerlinger, 1973). In addition, mathematical models and computer models are used to assess potential explanations (e.g., Townsend & Ashby, 1983). For many research problems, group designs that achieve control by averaging across subjects are regarded as the most appropriate. Results of research then are analyzed using established statistical procedures to determine whether the results can be attributed to something other than just chance.

In contrast, the Skinnerian view advocates almost exclusively the use of single-subject designs, regardless of the topic investigated (e.g., Johnston & Pennypacker, 1980; Sidman, 1960). In single-subject designs, control is not achieved by averaging across subjects but by comparing baseline and treatment conditions for individual subjects. This emphasis on single-subject designs is apparent in the *Journal of the Experimental Analysis of Behavior*, the primary basic research journal for TEAB. For example, a survey of the articles published between 1967 and 1969 showed that approximately 90% used single-subject designs (Bower & Hilgard, 1981). The large percentage of articles that use single-subject designs is hardly surprising, because a preference for such designs has been mandated in the journal's publication policy from the outset (Laties,

1987).

The rigid use of single-subject designs is prescribed in the primary, research-methods texts that take the behavior-analytic approach (Johnston & Pennypacker, 1980; Sidman, 1960). For example, Johnston and Pennypacker "regard the utility of group comparisons as extremely limited" (p. 89). According to those authors, "methods for studying behavior must isolate and identify the determinants of the individual's behavior, and experimental comparisons based on groups are *inappropriate by definition*" (p. 92, emphasis ours).

As part of their arguments for relying exclusively on single-subject designs, many behavior analysts also argue against the use of inferential statistics. Johnston and Pennypacker (1986) adopt this position, stating that "given the uniqueness of individual organisms and their past and present environmental interactions, any attempt to abbreviate the search for empirical generalities by collating the effects of the independent variable on the behavior of different subjects can only obfuscate rather than extend the relations of interest" (p. 30). In other words, Johnston and Pennypacker regard a difference between groups in an experiment that averages across subjects as "but a mathematical artifact" (p. 48).

4.6 ON THE USE OF THEORY

Most approaches to psychology emphasize the development of theory as the primary goal of research. In contrast, the behavior-analytic view minimizes the role of theory and sometimes is described as atheoretical.

According to Baars (1986), "psychological theory is more than unnecessary to Skinner; indeed it is impermissible. If a theory refers to the organism, it is physiology, not psychology. If it refers to something other than the organism, it is not physicalistic and therefore unscientific" (p. 67). Instead, behavior analysts prefer to describe functional relationships between variables (Johnston & Pennypacker, 1980; Skinner, 1953). These descriptions are of what the organism does and its relations to certain specifiable environmental conditions.

The characterization of the behavior-analytic view as atheoretical can be confusing, without a clear distinction between frameworks and theories (e.g., Anderson, 1983; Baars, 1986). According to

Anderson, "A framework is a general pool of constructs for understanding a domain, but it is not tightly enough organized to constitute a predictive theory" (p. 12). By this definition, reinforcement theory, which underlies TEAB, is classified more appropriately as a framework, as is the information-processing framework that guides much research in cognitive psychology. As Baars notes, "Because behaviorism is not a scientific theory but a presupposed framework, *it cannot be falsified by any experimental results*" (p. 52). Neither can the information-processing framework.

However, cognitive psychologists develop specific, predictive theories within the information-processing framework. These theories are used to generate hypotheses that then are tested experimentally. In contrast, behavior analysts are reluctant to develop predictive theories within the reinforcement framework. Rather, "in the area of behavioral research, the term hypothesis must be heavily qualified, for there are very few formal theories remaining that dictate singular experiments whose function is to confirm a hypothesis formally deduced from the theoretical corpus" (Johnston & Pennypacker, 1980, p. 38). Consequently, whereas the validity of the information-processing framework can be assessed by its fruitfulness in yielding formal, predictive theories (e.g., Marr, 1982), the validity of the reinforcement framework cannot be.

4.7 CONCLUSIONS

The preceding points demonstrate that TEAB differs from contemporary, scientific psychology in numerous fundamental respects. Given the overwhelming evidence that contemporary psychology is advancing rapidly, the question then becomes one of why behavior analysts persist in maintaining these differences. We propose that the answer is that the differences serve to aid in the pursuit of the goal of ensuring the survival of TEAB as a distinct discipline.

Because the goal is survival, rather than contributing to the science of psychology, the vast literature in the psychological sciences can be dismissed summarily as "unscientific" from a behavior-analytic point of view. As a consequence, the nature of what an experimental analysis of behavior should encompass can be redefined and, by definition, all alternative approaches classified as impotent to contribute to that science. The "legitimacy" of starting from scratch is maintained by asserting that psychology is unscientific and has made no progress (e.g., Harzem, 1987; Lee, 1988; Skinner, 1987).

The dismissal of all other approaches as unscientific is summarized vividly in a statement by George A. Miller, a major figure in the development of cognitive psychology. Miller attributes this statement to Herbert Jenkins, a past associate editor of the *Journal of Experimental Analysis of Behavior* and a former student of Skinner's:

> You know, you can learn Skinnerian psychology very quickly: The first day you're there, you learn that statistics is no damn good. Bang! like that. I don't have to worry about *that*. The next day you learn that physiological psychology is no damn good. Bang! just like that. You don't have to worry about it. The third day you learn that the history of psychology is no damn good. Bang! just like that, you've handled that. You go down any road until you come to Fred Skinner, and *that's* where psychology starts. It's really like that! (Baars, 1986, p. 206)

5

RELATION TO SCIENCE

The previous chapter indicates that one consequence of adopting the survival goal is that TEAB bears little resemblence to mainstream experimental psychology. A greater consequence is that this survival goal could be placed more basic than the goal of the scientific pursuit of knowledge. If so, TEAB would be precluded from sharing even a common conception of science with mainstream experimental psychology.

Though philosophical analyses lead to fluctuating views regarding the nature of science, there is wide agreement on certain basic principles. These principles provide the focus for the present section, because to the extent that any field of inquiry endeavors to attain scientific legitimacy, it must follow these basic principles. To assess whether TEAB adheres to these principles, and thus shares a common conception of science with mainstream experimental psychology, we consider in detail the behavior-analytic conception of science and the scientific practices of TEAB.

5.1 ON THE GOALS OF SCIENCE

The basic goal of science is theory, with subgoals including explanation, prediction, and control. Theories should generate new, testable hypotheses.

As indicated previously, behavior analysts typically argue against the use of theories (e.g., Skinner, 1950). Rather than attempting to test hypotheses deduced from predictive theories, behavior analysts prefer an "inductive strategy [that] forces the accumulation of facts" (Johnston & Pennypacker, 1980, p. 30). However, as noted by Kerlinger (1973), "Many people think that science is basically a fact-gathering activity. It is not" (p. 16). Instead, theories are derived to explain phenomena by specifying relevant variables and how and why they are related. The theories are general and apply to a range of situations.

The understanding that is derived from scientific theories facilitates accurate prediction and control. In this regard, it is interesting to note that behavior analysts typically describe the goals of science as including only prediction and control (e.g., Hayes & Brownstein, 1986; Johnston & Pennypacker, 1980; Skinner, 1953). Explanation and understanding are omitted because, "according to the behavior-analytic position, 'explanation' ultimately refers to prediction and control" (Hayes & Brownstein, 1986, p. 179). Yet, as Blough (1987) notes, "knowing how to control is not exactly the same as understanding how things work" (pp. 468-469).

Because, by their own admission (e.g., Johnston & Pennypacker, 1980), behavior analysts do not engage in testing hypotheses generated from precise theories, any finding can be interpreted in terms of the reinforcement framework. For example, Harzem and Miles (1978) state:

> Indeed, even if a sophisticated human subject set out in his responding to 'refute operant psychology' it is impossible as a matter of logic that he could ever

> do so. However he responded - for instance, if he pressed the lever at completely random time intervals without regard to the stimuli presented - it would still be possible to ask what were the conditions controlling such behaviour. (p. 83)

However, for Skinner, the analyses need not even meet the requirement of logical consistency:

> If it turns out that our final point of view of verbal behavior invalidates our scientific structure from the point of view of logic and truth-value, then so much the worse for logic, which will also have been embraced by our analysis. (Skinner, 1953, p. 594)

In summary, as Machan (1974) has noted, "It is clear that nothing could possibly count as an objection to Skinner" (p. 85) or to the basic assumptions that underlie TEAB.

5.2 ON EMPIRICAL EVIDENCE

The primary characteristic of science is systematic empiricism. Controlled observations are made of the phenomena of interest, and scientific explanations must be grounded in these observations.

Behavior analysts conduct empirical research. Because Skinner's position stresses the importance of environmental contingencies, most of the research is performed with nonhuman species, such as rats and pigeons (Fantino & Logan, 1979). Environmental contingencies are difficult for the experimenter to control in an open environment, thereby imposing considerable constraints on the knowledge that can be acquired from research on humans. Alternatively, through the use of contingency control in closed environments, which is possible with nonhuman species, these constraints are minimized.

Even though the basic operant-conditioning principles are grounded in research with animals, behavior analysts have a lengthy history of using these principles as evidence for their interpretations of human behavior (e.g., Skinner, 1948; 1953). MacKenzie (1977) notes that this extrapolation follows directly from assumptions that behavior analysts make regarding environmental and speciational generality:

> The assumption of environmental generality, to put it excessively crudely, asserts that the Skinner box is representative of all environments. The assumption of speciational generality, equally crudely, asserts that the pigeon is representative of all species of organisms. The two assumptions together provide a warrant for extrapolating from the behaviour of pigeons in Skinner boxes to the behaviour of all animals in all environments, and specifically to the behaviour of humans in complex social situations. (p. 160)

Indeed, Harzem and Williams (1983) describe the conditioning principles embodied in reinforcement theory as providing "an account of all aspects of human nature," even though "the empirical basis for the theory has arisen mainly from animal research" (p. 565).

Few studies have been conducted with the intent of verifying and generalizing the basic conditioning principles for normal human populations in controlled, laboratory settings, with most of this research having come only within the past several years (Buskist, 1987). These basic studies on the experimental analysis of human behavior (EAHB) have met with limited success, with many of the response profiles characteristic of infrahuman species not being obtained for the human population. H. L. Miller (1983), a behavior analyst, summarizes the situation as follows: "Despite consistent adherents (most notably Skinner), EAHB has had a checkered past, proceeding by fits and starts to its current position, where it may still be considered tenuous and fragmentary" (p. 552). As a consequence, "one is left to wonder whether EAHB is just dormant or is actually in the final abortive phases of demise" (p. 552).

In contrast to the relative lack of *basic* behavior-analytic research on humans, considerable *applied* research has been conducted on select human populations and on behavioral control in specific environments. This research met with some initial success and has led to the use of behavioral management techniques for prison populations, the institutionalized mentally retarded, industrial and educational environments, etc. The relative success of the applied research compared to the basic research with humans likely is a function of the previously mentioned minimization of constraints that occurs for closed environments. That is, the applied studies have been conducted with populations and/or environments that allow for the level of control that is necessary for effective behavioral management. However, because the applied research differs from the animal research in many ways, the effectiveness of the procedures may be for reasons other than those implied by the principles derived from the animal research (see, e.g., Schwartz & Lacey, 1982).

Current assessments by applied behavior analysts are relatively pessimistic, indicating that the initial successes in application of behavioral principles have not been extended in subsequent research. For example, Baer, Wolf, and Risley (1987) reach the paradoxical conclusion that "perhaps the clearest measure of our discipline's effectiveness is the increasing number of ineffective applications that we have tried in recent years" (p. 323). They go on to note that the failure rate has increased over the past 20 years and predict that "the next 20 almost surely will see that rate continue and, very likely, increase even more" (p. 324). Similarly, Kunkel (1987) notes that, in a comparison of the articles from the first volume of the *Journal of Applied Behavior Analysis* to those of the twentieth volume, it "certainly is not immediately apparent that 20 years have intervened. There appear to have been few if any basic changes in the major dimensions of applied behavior analysis" (p. 329). As a consequence, he concludes that "applied behavior analysis is in something of a rut" (pp. 329-330).

In sum, the behavioral principles derived from the animal research have not been verified to any great extent in the basic human research. Similarly, the applied extensions of those same principles to select human populations and environments have met with only limited success. Thus, in neither case is there a compelling empirical foundation from which to extend operant principles to account for human behavior.

5.3 ON THE TENTATIVE NATURE OF SCIENTIFIC KNOWLEDGE

In science, conclusions always are tentative. Because a useful scientific theory makes novel predictions, there is continuous interplay between theory and data. Theories are revised and replaced as new data become available.

Baars (1986) notes that the Skinnerian approach was developed primarily in the years 1930-1935 and has changed little since then. According to Baars, "Already in the 1930s Skinner wrote his friend Fred Keller that the battle for behaviorism would probably take several decades, but Skinner was willing to fight that long with *little doubt* that his cause was right, or of eventual victory" (p. 87, emphasis ours). Thus, from the outset, Skinner seems to have regarded his system as definitive, rather than tentative.

Guttman (1977) describes Skinner's writings as "exceptionally lucid, modest, and confident. The artfulness of Skinner's rhetoric seems...to be born of an inner confidence of the conceptions propounded, and nothing could be more persuasive" (p. 325). But by harboring a confidence that allowed for little doubt regarding his position, Skinner effectively ensured that subsequent empirical evidence would have little or no influence on his views. Confidence in one's views may be persuasive in an argument, and a lucid writing style may be of some value from a literary perspective, but these qualities have no bearing on the scientific validity of the claims.

The lack of interplay between data and theory is illustrated by Skinner's (1957) book, *Verbal Behavior*. This book presents a behavior-analytic interpretation of language acquisition and usage that Skinner (1978) asserts "will, I believe, prove to be my most important work" (p. 122). Indeed, a recent citation analysis showed that *Verbal Behavior* has had considerable impact, being referenced in 836 documents, as of 1984 (McPherson et al., 1984). However, only 19 of these citations involved experimental investigations, indicating that *Verbal Behavior* has had minimal impact on research. Thus, McPherson et al. conclude that, "for whatever reasons, *Verbal Behavior* has not provided a conception that has led to the empirical examination and explanation of verbal behavior" (p. 165). Similarly, Harzem and Williams (1983) note, "Skinner (1957) has provided a theoretical analysis of 'verbal behavior' which, it might be thought, would have firmly set the foundations for the development of a rich and detailed empirical analysis of language. It is curious, therefore, that so far rigorous research of that kind has not been forthcoming" (p. 571).

Additionally, the position taken in *Verbal Behavior* has been refuted soundly by linguists and psycholinguists, because it is primarily a speculative interpretation that fails to address the voluminous data on language acquisition and use (Chomsky, 1967). Yet, *Verbal Behavior* still is cited by behavior analysts as an often misunderstood work of major importance (e.g., Herrnstein, 1987; Winokur, 1976). *Verbal Behavior* illustrates vividly the problem of embracing a framework in the absence of empirical justification. The framework is still-born, leading to virtually no research, little revision, and, as a consequence, no systematic advances in knowledge.

The problem illustrated by *Verbal Behavior* also holds more generally for behavior-analytic accounts of human behavior. That is, the paucity of behavior-analytic research on human behavior likely is a consequence of the reinforcement framework being adopted as an account in advance of the data. Thus, although the principles embodied in the reinforcement framework enabled speculative solutions to many societal problems, these solutions remain primarily unsubstantiated inferences that are based predominantly on research with infrahumans (Machan, 1974).

While behavior analysts are willing to provide speculative interpretations of human behavior and to infer prescriptions for societal problems from a primarily non-human data base, they consider it inappropriate to draw inferences about underlying cognitive processes from behavioral data. For example, a description of the program in behavior analysis at a major university states, "If the so-called cognitive approaches are mistaken - and they are - the experimental analyst of behavior should be sufficiently equipped to know...why they are mistaken" (EAHB programs, 1983, p. 4). Moreover, behavior analysts often discuss the "dangers" inherent in the use of cognitive constructs (e.g., Liegland, 1984; Pennypacker, 1986). Yet, postulating entities that cannot be observed directly is a fundamental feature of science (Kerlinger, 1973; Machan, 1974; Stanovich, 1989). Most scientists clearly prefer data-based inferences over speculative interpretations that are far removed from the pertinent data.

5.4 ON THE ROLE OF PEER REVIEW AND EVALUATION

An important part of science is an open exchange of ideas. Close scrutiny and evaluation by fellow scientists enables alternative accounts of findings to be raised and evaluated, with scientific concepts progressively refined. Scientists are expected to publish their results in peer-reviewed journals within the discipline. This requirement ensures that authors are knowledgeable of the important findings and issues regarding the topic that is investigated and that reasonable standards of scholarship are met. Any major empirical finding or theory will be challenged when first published, with the ultimate level of acceptance depending on whether it can be defended against the challenges.

A general disregard for peer review and evaluation is evident in Skinner's training and career, as well as in the field of TEAB. In graduate school, Skinner's research was conducted "entirely without supervision" (Skinner, 1979, p. 35). According to Skinner,

> No one knew what I was doing until I handed in some kind of flimsy report. Possibly the psychologists thought I was being counseled by Crozier [his primary mentor at Harvard] and Hoagland [both physiologists], and they may have thought someone in psychology was

> keeping an eye on me, but the fact was that I was doing exactly as I pleased. (p. 35)

Skinner's doctoral thesis also did not have the benefit of supervision. In fact, it was largely a compilation of work that he already had in progress. The thesis was submitted to E. G. Boring, the noted historian of psychology, who indicated, among other things, that Skinner's review of the concept of reflex was "distorting history" (Skinner, 1979, p. 73). As a result, Boring twice recommended a complete revision, but Skinner refused to do so. At this point, Boring asked that the department appoint a committee and requested that he be left off. The committee subsequently approved the thesis.

It is important to note that the concerns expressed by Boring were not an isolated attack on Skinner. Rather, they reflected Boring's more general concern with the importance of having an accurate knowledge of historical foundations:

> The experimental psychologist, so it has always seemed to me, needs historical sophistication within his own sphere of expertness. Without such knowledge he sees the

> present in distorted perspective. He mistakes old facts and old views for new, and he remains unable to evaluate the significance of new movements. In this matter I can hardly state my faith too strongly. A psychological sophistication that contains no component of historical orientation seems to me to be no sophistication at all. (1950, ix)

Although Skinner's research during his early years at Harvard was unsupervised, he did publish numerous articles. In the introduction to Skinner's canonical papers, Catania (1984) notes that while at Harvard, Skinner "began a series of experiments that led to more than two dozen journal articles and culminated in *The Behavior of Organisms* (1938)" (p. 473). In fact, Skinner published 30 articles during this period, the majority (20) of which appeared in the *Journal of General Psychology*. Skinner (1979) characterizes these early works as "not in the mainstream of American psychology" (p. 178); this characterization is accurate, in that the works were relatively unreferenced and were published in minimally refereed outlets. For example, Skinner states that the reason for publishing the majority of his work in the *Journal of General Psychology* was that "the editor accepted almost anything submitted by a long list of associates" (p. 75).

The associate editor who submitted Skinner's articles was W. J. Crozier, Skinner's primary mentor. An example of Crozier's editorial scrutiny and judgment is provided in Skinner's autobiography (Skinner, 1979). Skinner relates the events surrounding a paper that he wrote for a course taught by Crozier. Skinner characterizes this paper as an "ill-tempered piece," of which he was not proud, that criticized an article by E. M. Vicari. Yet, Crozier made an editorial decision that "the paper should be published and sent it off to the *Journal of General Psychology*" (p. 46). The apparent motive underlying the determination to publish this and other manuscripts of Skinner's is that Crozier "was proud of the number of papers issued from his department" (p. 46). In summary, although Skinner had published more than two-dozen articles prior to 1938, they were published with minimal scrutiny in outlets that were not in the mainstream of psychological research. Moreover, the articles were primarily loosely documented, non-integrative reports in which only descriptions of the behavior of "typical" subjects were presented.

Skinner's empirical work gained prominence with the publication in 1938 of his book, *The Behavior of Organisms*. This book was a compilation and synthesis of the research presented in his prior publications. Although Skinner continued to publish articles after 1938, the empirical component in these works decreased substantially. The primary empirical contribution subsequently made by Skinner also was published in the form of a book, *Schedules of Reinforcement* (Ferster & Skinner, 1957), with the majority of the research described in the book not having been reported in journal format. Thus, most of Skinner's empirical work never underwent the systematic scrutiny of peer evaluation that occurs for articles published in major, peer-reviewed journals.

Many early developments in the field of TEAB indicate that the apparent lack of appreciation for the peer review process demonstrated by Skinner was carried over into the field as a whole. As stressed previously, very little of the research of behavior analysts is published in standard psychology journals. Instead, the research is published in what at least one behavior analyst characterizes as "in-house journal[s]" (Buskist, 1987, p. 1), such as the *Journal of Applied Behavior Analysis* and the *Journal of the Experimental Analysis of Behavior*, which are "essentially the house organ[s] of the operant conditioning movement" (Bower & Hilgard, 1981, p. 209). Thus, the "close scrutiny" of behavior analysts' research comes primarily from other behavior analysts and not from a broader range of psychologists.

The reason often given for the founding of the *Journal of the Experimental Analysis of Behavior* is that the editorial process in psychology journals was creating an obstacle that precluded publication of behavior-analytic work (e.g., Kelleher & Morse, 1987; Skinner, 1983a). However, Laties (1987), a former editor of the *Journal of the Experimental Analysis of Behavior*, emphasizes that "the difficulties that operant conditioners faced in publishing their findings are somewhat overdrawn" (p. 497). Indeed, the major figures in behavior-analytic research had numerous articles published in reputable psychology and scientific journals during the years immediately preceding the founding of the *Journal of the Experimental Analysis of Behavior*.

Laties notes that the founding editor of

the journal, Charles Ferster, "had since 1951 published three papers in the *Journal of Experimental Psychology*, two in *Science*, one each in *Psychological Bulletin*, *Psychological Monographs*, *Psychiatric Research Reports*, and the *Harvard Educational Review*" (p. 497). Similarly, Brady (1987) indicates that he "had published several papers during the mid- and early-1950s in what was then perhaps the high-prestige journal of its time -- the *Journal of Comparative and Physiological Psychology*" (p. 458). In fact, Brady subsequently served as a member of the journal's editorial board. Another major researcher in TEAB, Schoenfeld (1987), states that although others were finding it difficult getting their work published in the journals of the American Psychological Association, he "was not having such difficulties" (p. 465). Thus, editorial policies were not preventing sound, behavior-analytic research from being published in psychology journals.

Instead of the *Journal of the Experimental Analysis of Behavior* being started because of unfairness in the editorial policies of the psychology journals, it appears to have been founded primarily to enable behavior analysts to circumvent the editorial process. Yet, it is this editorial process that serves to maintain the integrity of the journals, through the scientific rigor demanded by the editorial consultants. That scientific rigor was considered to be a hindrance is captured by Dews (1987), who describes himself and other behavior analysts as being "too busy making discoveries to be willing to divert long hours to the preparation of proper scientific papers" (p. 461).

The intent to circumvent the editorial process is illustrated by a 1956 letter from Charles Ferster to William H. Morse that presaged the founding of the *Journal of the Experimental Analysis of Behavior*. In that letter, Ferster suggested that he, along with Morse and others, should send their best work to a small-circulation newsletter, the *Psychological Newsletter*, because the editor "will publish it unedited" (Kelleher & Morse, 1987, p. 456). One reason Ferster gave for wanting to publish his papers "unedited" was to avoid "the damaging subtle audience control that takes place when I write an article for [Harry] Harlow or [Arthur] Melton [who were editors of American Psychological Association journals at the time]" (p. 456).

Apparently, then, the intent behind the founding of the *Journal of the Experimental Analysis of Behavior* was for behavior analysts to avoid having to prepare well-written reports that related their research to the larger body of psychological literature. The lack of appreciation for the editorial process that is apparent in Ferster's letter manifested itself in his subsequent editorial policy for the journal, which was "that poor or unreadable papers did not really hurt a journal" (Dews, 1987, p. 461).

In general, criticisms from individuals outside of TEAB concerning the research of behavior analysts typically are regarded as unjustified and repressive. For example, Johnston and Pennypacker (1980) state, "The most conspicuous opponents of the science of behavior are the social scientists; their opposition illuminates their function as custodians of the traditional knowledge base with which society attempts to manage itself" (p. 19). Johnston and Pennypacker describe Skinner's original research as drawing "immediate and sustained criticism from the whole spectrum of the social sciences" (p. 17). According to Johnston and Pennypacker, this critical discourse "is only the most recent manifestation of the historically inevitable reaction of a surrounding culture to an important scientific advance" (p. 18). Nowhere in their discussion do Johnston and Pennypacker acknowledge that careful scrutiny of new proposals is part of the scientific method and that scientists would be remiss if they did not challenge new proposals of any type.

5.5 SUMMARY

Although behavior analysts maintain that TEAB is *the* science of behavior, they stand largely in disagreement with many of the conventional principles and practices of science. Behavior analysts minimize the importance of empirical evidence, exclude explanation from the "behavior-analytic conception of science," and denigrate the role of peer review and evaluation. Thus, the goal of ensuring the survival of TEAB as a distinct discipline has led behavior analysts to re-conceptualize the nature of science. Given that the other facet of the behavior-analytic goal is to ensure the adoption of their views, it would not be surprising to find that behavior analysts engage in many activities that are consistent with characteristics of pseudoscience. We present evidence of such activities in the next chapter.

6

RELATION TO PSEUDOSCIENCE

To this point, we have summarized evidence that places TEAB at variance with both the conventional practices of scientific psychology and the rational principles of science. Our contention is that these deviations are a consequence of behavior analysts having the primary goal of ensuring the adoption and survival of TEAB as a distinct discipline. We further suggest that behavior analysts engage in a range of extraneous activities as acceptable means to accomplish this goal.

Without the safeguards invoked when the scientific pursuit of knowledge is the primary goal, these extraneous activities can vary considerably in terms of their scientific validity. The following section describes several of the specific features of pseudoscience, which are taken from several sources (Cazeau & Scott, 1979; Gardner, 1957; Radner & Radner, 1982; Thagard, 1988), and provides evidence for their existence in many of the activities of behavior analysts.

6.1 ON BEING RELIANT ON A SINGLE, PRIMARY INDIVIDUAL

A pseudoscience forms a cult following around a charismatic individual who serves as the spiritual leader for the followers.

B. F. Skinner is the individual who serves the role of spiritual leader for TEAB, with this role exemplified in several ways. First, he is the only individual around whom a division of the American Psychological Association (Division 25) is devoted (Guttman, 1977; Landers, 1988). Second, approximately half of the articles published in the *Journal of the Experimental Analysis of Behavior* refer to one or more works of Skinner. In contrast, he is referenced no more than a couple of times a year in the volumes of the *Journal of Experimental Psychology* (Guttman, 1977). Third, articles by behavior analysts characterize Skinner as "standing alone" in relation to the rest of psychology (e.g., Harzem, 1987) and often are dedicated to him (e.g., Baron, Kaufman, & Stauber, 1969; Harzem, 1987). In fact, a published Festschrift for Skinner (Dews, 1970), which consisted primarily of articles from volume 12 of the *Journal of the Experimental Analysis of Behavior*, stated that the criterion for inclusion was that the article be dedicated to Skinner. Fourth, and perhaps most indicative of Skinner's role as a spiritual icon, limited-edition portraits, signed by Skinner and the artist, are advertised for purchase in the newsletter published by the Association for Behavior Analysis (*The ABA Newsletter*, spring, 1988, p. 17).

Irving Maltzman, a non-Skinnerian behaviorist, attributes Skinner's success as a spiritual leader to his charisma. "He's got character, charisma, he's an enormous egoist - which you need in order to be a charismatic individual - and he developed a following. It's like a religion" (Baars, 1986, p. 103). Ernest Hilgard, a respected historian of psychology, elaborates further the religious nature of Skinnerian behaviorism:

> I suppose that it's almost like

> religious commitment. Think for instance of Skinner, of being just so committed to this thing that to his disciples he's just like a god. His early disciple was Fred Keller. They were graduate students together at Harvard....Fred is almost a St. Paul, except that Skinner didn't need a St. Paul to promulgate his theory. He was his own Paul, so I don't know; John the Baptist maybe is a better designation for Fred Keller. (Baars, 1986, p. 292)

It is important to stress that Skinner's role as the spiritual leader of TEAB is not a chance event. Rather, the late Norman Guttman, a student of Skinner's, emphasizes that Skinner "*has intended that it be so* through the philosophical writings (Skinner, 1971, 1974) to which he has devoted most of his recent energies" (Guttman, 1977, p. 323; emphasis ours). Guttman depicts his mentor's role as a spiritual leader in a way on which we cannot improve:

> Skinner has become a symbol; he has become more than himself. Skinner is, as it were, the leading

> figure in a myth, a myth already made in the popular imagination and awaiting a new occupant. He has succeeded to the role of the scientist-hero, the Promethean fire-bringer, the master technologist and instructor of technologists. Also, his is the role of the chief iconoclast, the image-breaker who liberates our thoughts from ancient restrictions. To this composite role Skinner adds the unique personal element of encouragement, reinforcement, kindness, love - which he presents as a universal message based, at long last, on a scientific foundation. To several audiences before..., I have suggested that Skinner could be characterized as a unique combination of the figures of Thomas A. Edison, Jesus Christ, and Bertrand Russell, and I stand by that characterization here. (pp. 322-323)

6.2 ON APPEALING TO MYTHICAL TALES

Pseudoscientists often develop mythical tales

to which they appeal in order to give their case credibility.

A mythical air surrounds many of the writings of Skinner and other behavior analysts. The best example is Skinner's (1948) novel, *Walden Two*, which is an entirely fictional account of a Utopian community based on reinforcement principles. The book also reflects "a venture in self therapy," in which Skinner was "struggling to reconcile two aspects of [his] own behavior" (Skinner, 1982, p. 26). The struggle was whether to be solely a scientist or also a futuristic prophet with the mission of re-structuring society. This struggle is played out in the novel by two main characters, *Burris*, an academic scholar, and *Frazier*, the founder of the Utopian community of Walden Two. At the conclusion of the novel, Burris joins Frazier in Walden Two, thus reflecting Skinner's resolution of his personal struggle with the decision to be a futuristic prophet. The mixing of science and mythology, as in *Walden Two*, blurs the distinction between scientific fact and fiction. For example, Harzem and Williams (1983) attribute the beginnings of the broader socio-political implications of reinforcement theory to that novel. Moreover, even today, when discussing psychological issues and societal problems, Skinner refers to the commune of Walden Two as if it were a real, functioning community. According to him, "*Walden Two* is an *experiment* in the design of a *social* environment" (Skinner, 1978, p. 9; emphasis on "experiment" is ours). Moreover, in describing what he characterizes as a piecemeal approach taken by modern psychotherapies not based on TEAB, Skinner stresses that Walden Two attempted to solve the problems of society "all at once rather than one by one" (Buie, 1988, p. 21).

When asked by Masterson (1988) whether he regrets not having lived in Twin Oaks, a community modeled after *Walden Two*, or in another such community, Skinner responded that he does not, because "they are too small. *Walden Two* was a thousand people. Twin Oaks is about a hundred and I think that you would see the same faces a little too often" (p. 1). But, there were no "real" faces in *Walden Two*, nor were there any "real" problems solved. Consequently, a story with a "happy ending" cannot serve as scientific evidence. Such a blurring of scientific fact and fiction is inherently dangerous in that it can lead to prescriptions for the solutions to *real* societal and psychological problems that are made in the name of science, but without genuine scientific support.

Even Skinner's more serious, scholarly endeavors have the character of mythical tales, because the endeavors primarily are speculative interpretations. For example, Chomsky (1967) characterizes Skinner's account of language acquisition and usage in *Verbal Behavior* as a mythical tale. Chomsky notes that, "the conclusion that I hoped to establish [in his famous review of the book] was that the general point of view is largely mythology" (p. 142). Despite the fact that *Verbal Behavior* has had little influence on psychology or linguistics, because it is largely speculative, Skinner regards that book and the entirely fictional novel, *Walden Two*, as two of his three greatest contributions (Masterson, 1988).

Perhaps the greatest myth perpetuated by behavior analysts concerns the scientific status of reinforcement theory. According to Harzem and Williams (1983), "Reinforcement theory [is] the outstanding scientific theory of human behavior in the present century," and "is now the one all-encompassing theory of behavior" (p. 567). This sweeping claim is made despite the fact that, by their own assessment, "empirical evidence bearing on it....has not, so far, been readily forthcoming" (p. 567). Without being based on a solid foundation of empirical evidence, a theory is not scientific but is a myth.

6.3 ON RESPONDING TO CRITICISM

Pseudoscientists pride themselves on never having been shown to be wrong. Their views change little, and criticisms raised by others often are dismissed summarily as being based on a failure to understand the position.

Despite the major advances that have occurred since the 1930s in psychology, Skinner's system has remained largely unchanged (Baars, 1986). In an interview with Skinner, Baars noted it has been suggested that Skinner's polemical style led him to adopt extreme positions from which he never escaped. Skinner's response was, in part, that "the claims I have made seem to me to have been borne out. There has been criticism - sometimes vicious criticism - of *Beyond Freedom and Dignity* (1971). But certainly the formulation of the operant and of reinforcement has held up remarkably well. Research and basic analysis go straight ahead" (p. 92).

A specific case of refusing to respond constructively to criticism involves Chomsky's (1959) critique of Skinner's (1957) *Verbal Behavior*. This critique played a major role in convincing psychologists that behavior-analytic principles are inadequate for explaining human language. Yet, Skinner never responded in print to the critique, stating some eight years afterward that "I have never actually read more than a dozen pages of Chomsky's famous review of *Verbal Behavior*" (Skinner, 1982, p. 31). His reason for not reading further was that Chomsky had misunderstood the intent of *Verbal Behavior* (Skinner, 1983a, p. 153).

The theme that Skinner's works are misunderstood by most scientific psychologists and other behavioral and social scientists runs throughout behavior-analytic writings. In the introduction to Skinner's canonical papers, Catania (1984) characterizes Skinner as "the most misrepresented" and "most misunderstood" (p. 473) of all contemporary psychologists. Behavior analysts lament this misunderstanding in their evaluations of arguments made by Skinner's critics. For example, Hinson (1987) states that "unfortunately many psychologists and philosophers have a difficult time understanding radical behaviorism" (p. 204). Similarly, Richelle

(1987) argues that "many aspects of Skinner's thinking have been persistently misinterpreted by his opponents" (p. 127). The implication is that if Skinner's views were understood, these views would be justly acknowledged by the community of scientific psychologists.

6.4 ON A PARANOID STYLE

Pseudoscientists consider themselves to be geniuses and regard their colleagues as ignorant. They believe themselves to be persecuted and focus their attacks on the greatest scientists and the best-established theories.

Meissner (1978) describes several elements of the paranoid style: (1) displacement of responsibility from the self to others; (2) suspiciousness of others; (3) grandiosity; (4) delusional fixity and conviction of the reality of the delusion; (5) creation of a fictional, "paranoid pseudocommunity" (Cameron, 1943), in which unrelated persons and groups are organized into a fantasized community that is perceived as posing a threat to the paranoid individual; and (6) a restructuring of cognitive processes to form a meaningful interpretive system into which each new input is assimilated. Each of these elements can be found consistently throughout the writings and activities of behavior analysts and are evident in many of the quotations and citations presented previously in this book.

Most importantly, it should be clear to the reader that in answering the question of why TEAB has not <u>become</u> psychology, Skinner (1987) elected to displace responsibility from himself and the other behavior analysts to the unjust "formidable obstacles" created by other psychologists. In doing so, the simple dichotomy that Skinner sets up between behavior analysts and "others" treats as a homogeneous "pseudocommunity" many psychologists who take quite disparate approaches to the study of human behavior, while ignoring their considerable heterogeneity.

To convey a sense of the pervasiveness of the paranoid elements in the writings of behavior analysts, we provide the following additional examples. The establishment of a paranoid pseudocommunity is evident in the following quotation by Fraley and Vargas (1986):

> Professional psychologists in

> psychology departments and out, sort themselves out into two camps: The overwhelming majority who are developmentalists, Freudians, Rogerians, so-called humanists, information theorists, brain-mind epiphenomenalists, and so on - in short, cognitivists of all sorts - and, submerged among them, a small minority of behaviorists. (p. 49)

Having established a fantasized pseudocommunity of people outside of TEAB, behavior analysts typically attribute the shortcomings of TEAB to the actions of this pseudocommunity. According to Lamal (1988), some behavior analysts are pessimistic about the likelihood that the radical behavior program will contribute much more to the solution of important social problems, yet "the reason for the pessimism is not the inadequacy of the behavioral program but the resistance of nonbehaviorists" (p. 178). Indeed, Fraley and Vargas (1986) assert:

> The ideological fervor of eclectic balance in the academic factory requires that any minority view be suppressed....Although minority practitioners might refine a

> principle and the practices based upon it, both in their work and in the publications they control, the majority tends to ignore it until one or more of its members can find a way through the work *they* do, to discover and refine the same principle in *their* work and in *their* literature and speak of it in *their* terms. (pp. 49-50)

Fraley and Vargas (1986) then provide a specific example through an attack on Amos Tversky, who was awarded the McArthur prize and the 1983 American Psychological Association award for distinguished scientific contributions. The latter award was for innovative ways of studying and theorizing about decision making and preference. But, according to Fraley and Vargas, Tversky's insightful research is little more than a restatement, albeit in cognitive terms, of Skinner's (1953, 1969) discussions of the topics. Fraley and Vargas describe the example of Tversky versus Skinner as illustrating...

> the operating style whereby the political majority appropriates control of the knowledge base,

> insures control over professional recognitions, the acclaim, the enhanced opportunities, and even the wealth (the McArthur award included $232,000 in cash), which all funnel to that political majority. The technically advanced minority remains a band of ignored or used persons whose ideas are rediscovered or adopted and then promoted as new intellectual merchandise. (p. 51)

6.5 ON ANACHRONISTIC THINKING

Pseudoscientists often advocate views that once were considered to be promising, but that subsequently have been rejected in the light of empirical data. These anachronistic views continue to be held even though new evidence to justify their reconsideration is not put forth.

The predominant framework in psychology during the 1940s was Hullian behaviorism, a form of behaviorism that attempted to provide precise, quantified theories of learning and performance. The theories relied on the use of hypothetical mechanisms to mediate between stimuli and responses (Hilgard, 1987). In the early 1950s, psychology entered a period of crisis when it became evident that Hullian theory was not capable of accounting adequately for behavior. One alternative to Hullian behaviorism was the reinforcement framework of TEAB, which minimized the use of theory based on hypothetical mechanisms. Another alternative was the information-processing framework.

During the ensuing years, the latter framework has proved to be fruitful in enabling psychologists to address a broader range of psychological topics than was possible previously. Moreover, progress in psychology has coincided with the progress in related sciences, such as computer science, artificial intelligence, linguistics, and industrial engineering, culminating in the establishment of interdisciplinary cognitive-science educational and research programs in the 1980s. The advances in these disciplines have alleviated many of the concerns about mentalistic accounts that were raised by Skinner and his followers (see, e.g., L. Miller, 1988). Yet, despite these advances, and despite the self-admitted relative lack of progress in understanding human behavior within the reinforcement framework (e.g., H. L. Miller, 1983), behavior analysts persist in advocating the directives and restrictions regarding research and theory proposed by Skinner in his formative years (see, e.g., Harzem, 1987).

Behavior analysts characterize their views as representing the new scientific approach, whereas alternative views are archaic and pre-scientific (e.g., Johnston & Pennypacker, 1980). Yet, Machan (1974) stresses that "basically what Skinner does is simply reiterate a philosophy of nature which has been with us at least since Democritus" (p. 80) and "Leucippus, both of whom propounded a strictly materialistic conception of nature. Since these views, as well as later ones, are not appreciably different from Skinner's, the latter cannot sustain his point about the modernity of his own ideas" (p. 59).

6.6 ON IRREFUTABLE HYPOTHESES AND EXPLANATION BY SCENARIO

Scientific hypotheses must be refutable. That is, they must be empirically testable. To explain a phenomenon scientifically is to show how it follows from general laws. Without laws there is only a tale that does not have a proper scientific foundation. Pseudoscientific hypotheses and theories usually are not testable, and interpretations derived from them often involve ad hoc scenarios.

The reinforcement framework can be used to interpret any novel behaviors by attributing those behaviors to the reinforcement history of the individual. But these interpretations are ad hoc scenarios that are untestable. As Baars (1986) notes, "No one actually searches back to see what it was, in the history of the organism, that produced some current behavior. But referring to the 'history of the organism' permits Skinner to claim that one could do this *in principle*" (p. 63). The important point is that whereas knowledge of an organism's reinforcement history can be used to predict behavior in controlled, laboratory settings, similar historical knowledge is not available for humans. Thus, interpretations of most human behaviors necessarily are ad hoc.

Skinner characterizes his writings about human behavior as *interpretations*. For example, *Verbal Behavior* was "an exercise in interpretation" (1973, p. 261), in which he noted similarities between reinforcement contingencies that promote verbal behavior and the contingencies that have been analyzed with greater precision for lower organisms in the laboratory. Skinner indicates that *Beyond Freedom and Dignity* also was "an exercise in interpretation" (p. 261). He emphasizes that the science lies behind, rather than in, these writings.

For Skinner, the criticisms of his interpretations rest "on the existence, or at least the eminence, of a science of behavior. I believe that such a science exists, but I made no effort to prove it. I assumed that my readers would either look up the references at the end of the book or take my word for it for the sake of argument" (1973, p. 257). In other words, Skinner's critics did not find proof for a science of behavior in *Verbal Behavior* or *Beyond Freedom and Dignity*, because the proof was not there. Similarly, those who agree with Skinner's interpretations also must assume that the pertinent scientific evidence exists somewhere (Machan, 1974).

6.7 ABUSE OF FACTS AND LOGIC

Pseudoscientific writings often include factual error, distortion or exaggeration, contradiction, innuendo, ad hominem argument, failure to specify, speculation, hasty generalization, appeal to pity, and appeal to authority.

The previous sections include many examples of abuses of facts and logic. Additional examples are given in the present section. Factual error, distortion, and exaggeration are present in many of the writings of behavior analysts. For example, Harzem's (1987) call for a return to operant behaviorism contains numerous factual errors and distortions regarding the state of contemporary psychology (Proctor & Weeks, 1988). Similarly, Johnston and Pennypacker's (1980) statement that "our need for a scientific understanding of the determinants of human behavior has been almost totally unfulfilled during the past 150 years" (p. 92) is a misrepresentation of the progress that has occurred within scientific psychology.

Contradiction also can be found in the writings of behavior analysts. For example, when discussing why he failed to reply to Chomsky's (1959) critique of *Verbal Behavior*, Skinner asserts that he has "*never* been interested in critical reactions, either positive or negative" (1967, p. 31; emphasis ours). Yet, he indicates elsewhere that when he was provided the opportunity to reply to Joseph Wood Krutch, a critic of *Walden Two*,

"I was happy to take the opportunity to answer Krutch and review the implications" (1982, p. 151). It would seem logical that Skinner would be equally willing to respond to Chomsky as he was to respond to Krutch. These contradictory statements raise the question of why not.

A similar contradiction in logic arises in the acceptance of behavior analysis as a world view. Specifically, how can it be that Skinner has the capacity to choose for all of us the correct manner in which to view the nature of humans, whereas the rest of us are under the control of the contingencies of our environment and have no similar freedom of choice (Machan, 1974)?

Innuendo and ad hominem attacks also appear frequently in the TEAB literature. A good illustration is Pennypacker's (1986) discussion, in his Presidential Address to the Association for Behavior Analysis, of the need for behavioral training in American industry. According to Pennypacker, "American industry is prepared to spend vast sums of money to improve training of its workforce....it is also prepared to lavish these resources on the so-called cognitive sciences. *I need not tell you* what the consequences of that misjudgement will be, either for our discipline or for our culture" (pp. 154-155; emphasis ours). Pennypacker uses the derogatory term "so called" to refer to the cognitive sciences and characterizes support of them as a "misjudgement", but provides no concrete information on which the reader can assess the validity of the statement. Similar ad hominem attacks by innuendo are made on individuals, such as that of Fraley and Vargas (1986) on Amos Tversky that was described earlier.

Failure to specify is captured in the ad hoc argument that a behavior is maintained through a person's "reinforcement history", which never can be known in its entirety. Speculation and hasty generalization are apparent in the willingness of Skinner and others to generalize their results obtained primarily with nonhuman species to the solution of educational problems, socio-political problems, and behavior problems for individuals (e.g., Skinner, 1953).

Finally, appeals to pity resonate through many of the writings of behavior analysts (e.g., Epstein, 1984; Fraley & Vargas, 1986), in their insistence that they are not receiving their "just rewards". Moreover, as should be apparent from the descriptions provided earlier, essentially all major issues are appealed to the authority of B. F. Skinner.

6.8 SUMMARY

Many of the activities of behavior analysts that we have described in this chapter do not make much sense if viewed in isolation. Moreover, if examined from the traditional scientific perspective, these activities remain nonsensical. In fact, they fulfill many of the features of pseudoscience. However, when regarded as but means to fulfill the goal of ensuring the adoption and survival of TEAB as a distinct discipline, the actions are sensible. That is, placing the goals of science secondary to the goal of TEAB removes the restraints provided by the scientific method, thereby allowing virtually any activity to be regarded as justifiable.

PART III

IMPLICATIONS AND FUTURE PROSPECTS

7

THE PARADOX OF BEHAVIOR ANALYSIS

The evidence in support of a distinction between the goals of scientific psychology and of TEAB enables a resolution to the paradox of why Skinner's system has had considerable impact outside of scientific psychology but not inside. The present chapter examines the paradox and presents the resolution.

7.1 LIMITED IMPACT OF TEAB WITHIN SCIENTIFIC PSYCHOLOGY

As a consequence of having a separate goal, virtually all of the basic tenets of mainstream psychological research are denied by behavior analysts, despite the fact that these tenets have been developed from over 100 years of intensive investigation (see, e.g., Posner, 1982, and Rescorla, 1988). Behavior analysts hold that the research methods used by psychologists are inappropriate, that psychological theory cannot be based on inferred events, and that research should involve primarily an inductive gathering of facts instead of hypotheses derived deductively from theories. These claims are in direct contradiction to the substantial body of basic and applied knowledge that has been acquired in psychology using the conventional methods.

The behavior-analytic system clearly stands on the fringe of scientific psychology. Skinner formed the system without the benefit of broad exposure to psychology and made little attempt to integrate it with the field. Moreover, most of the research conducted by other behavior analysts also has been outside of mainstream psychology. Thus, Skinner and the other behavior analysts simply have operated outside of the system of psychological science.

Although Skinner has a respectable publication record, including some articles in mainstream psychology journals, the majority of his published works are non-research based. This point is illustrated by

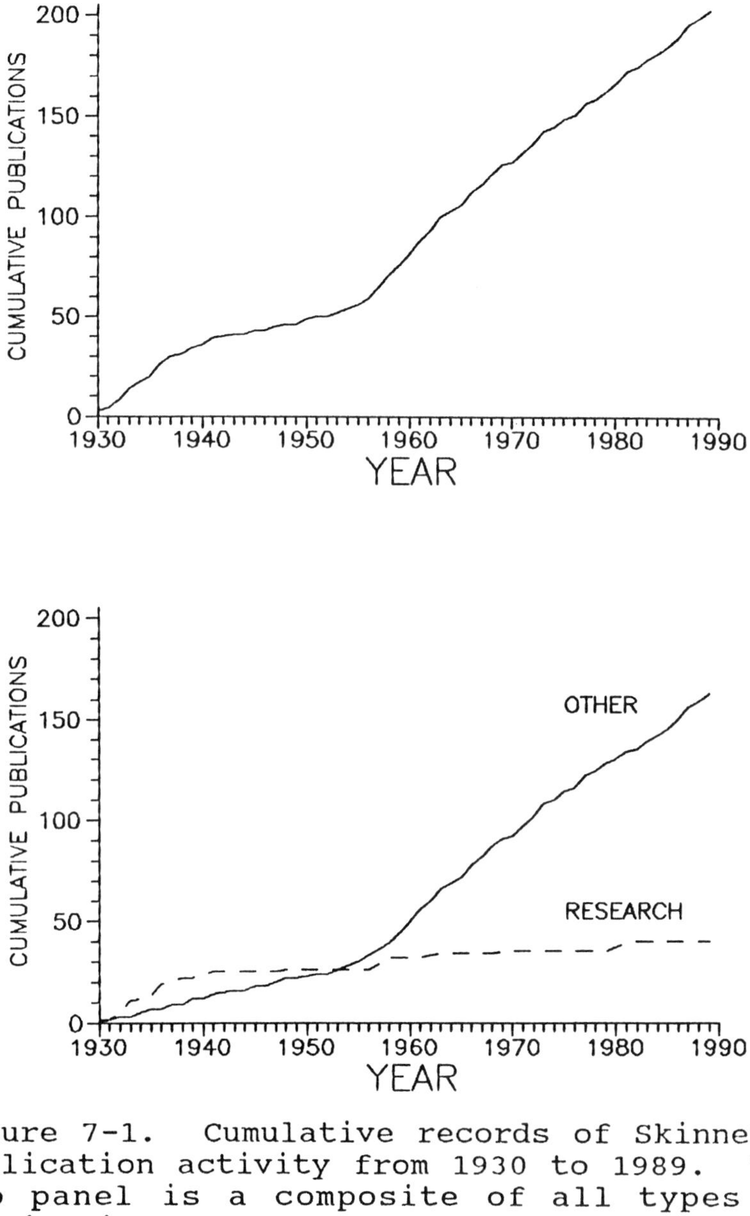

Figure 7-1. Cumulative records of Skinner's publication activity from 1930 to 1989. The top panel is a composite of all types of publications. The bottom panel decomposes the function into separate records for research reports and other types of publications.

the cumulative records of Skinner's publication behavior presented in Figure 7-1. The top panel, which is adapted from Epstein (1982) and extended through 1989, is the cumulative record of Skinner's published papers and books. Epstein describes this record as showing "a high, steady stable rate of publishing over most of Skinner's 50-year career in psychology" (p. 6).

Although Epstein's description is accurate, a different picture emerges when the publication record is decomposed into its constituent behaviors. Specifically, the bottom panel of Figure 7-1 plots separately the cumulative records for scientific research reports and for other types of publications. This decomposition shows clearly that the two component publication behaviors display quite different functions. The record for scientific research reports shows a rapid rise from 1930 to 1938, which reflects the research activity that led to the *Behavior of Organisms*. From 1938 to the present, the record shows only a slight slope, which reflects the fact that the number of published research reports in the ensuing 50 years is approximately equal to that in the initial 8 years. In contrast, the record for other publications is a positively accelerated function. Thus, the empirical component contributes little to the composite function after 1938, with the continued growth of that function being determined almost entirely by works that are not scientific research reports.

The evidence also indicates that many of the activities of Skinner and other behavior analysts do not adhere to the rational principles of science. First, behavior analysts regard predictive theories as of little value, particularly as they pertain to the development of research questions. Second, they place relatively little emphasis on empirical confirmation of their interpretations of behavior. Third, they give little credence to statistical confirmation of the descriptive summaries of their data. Finally, they show disregard for the evaluation and confirmation provided by the peer review process.

In addition to the deviations from psychology and science, the activities of Skinner and the behavior analysts show many of the features of pseudoscience. First, TEAB has formed around a single, charismatic individual. Second, a dogmatic, mythical structure has been developed that blurs fact and fiction. Third, behavior analysts regard themselves as persecuted, with the criticisms typically attributed to a failure to understand the behavior-analytic position. The picture that emerges is that, despite public perceptions, TEAB simply is not synonomous with scientific psychology.

7.2 EXTENSIVE IMPACT OF TEAB OUTSIDE OF SCIENTIFIC PSYCHOLOGY

The impact of TEAB outside of scientific psychology has been great for several reasons. First, as Figure 7-1 shows, the larger component of Skinner's publication behavior has involved non-research articles, most of which were targeted for psychological practitioners, social scientists and educators outside of psychology, and the lay public. Second, Skinner's writings claim that a strong, scientific foundation for the behavior-analytic principles exists, and the members of the target readerships simply are not in a position to evaluate such a claim.

It is also important to note that Skinner formulated his system at a point in his career at which he admittedly was not broadly knowledgeable regarding psychology. Given that Skinner formulated the system largely from the standpoint of a layman, it is not surprising that the core concepts that form the language of its interpretations are relatively simple and easy to grasp. These core concepts enable even a lay individual to provide unsophisticated "interpretations", veiled in science, for virtually all behaviors. Finally, the behavior-analytic system has been couched in terms of its affinity to the theories of evolution and natural selection, which have unparalleled esteem in the lay community. The evidence, thus, indicates that the impact of Skinner's views outside of scientific psychology arise at least in part because they provide a simple "parsimonious" world view that is vigorously promoted to the public "in the name of science".

7.3 MISUNDERSTANDING

As indicated previously, behavior analysts state that critics misunderstand Skinner's views. Some misunderstandings do in fact exist. However, Malone (1987b) notes that Skinner also "has been misinterpreted by sympathetic colleagues of long standing" (p. 194). Among these colleagues are former students and members of the editorial board for the *Journal of the Experimental Analysis of Behavior*. Malone (1987a) also characterizes a recent "future directions" issue of that journal as being "depressing" (p. 206), because contributors misunderstood the basic premises of TEAB. Interestingly, he concludes that "these depressing recent developments" are attributable to Skinner: "Skinner's lack of consistency has fostered the confusion that has led to them" (p. 206).

That Skinner was inconsistent in his writings suggests that he may have misunderstood the critical aspects of his arguments, as well. This is the conclusion that Malone (1987a) reaches, emphasizing that "Skinner's best ideas are difficult to understand (even for him)" (p. 206). As one specific example, Malone (1987b) notes that interpretations provided by Skinner in Chapter 2 of the *Behavior of Organisms* could not have been made by anyone "who understood the preceding chapter" (p. 198). Given that Skinner and other behavior analysts have difficulty understanding the behavior-analytic system, it is of little wonder that non-behavior analysts "misunderstand" the system. In short, it seems unlikely that even the most well-intentioned, careful, and knowledgeable reader could interpret Skinner's writings "correctly".

7.4 SKINNER'S INTERPRETATIONS

One major misunderstanding of Skinner's writings arises from their nature. That is, the writings have been scrutinized from both scientific and philosophical perspectives and found to be lacking. Yet, Skinner has gone to great lengths to make the point that his writings are neither science nor philosophy. Rather, he characterizes all of his major books on human behavior as *interpretations*. Similarly, he also classifies his canonical papers (Catania, 1984) as interpretations.

Fortunately, Skinner leaves little room for misunderstanding what he means by the term "interpretation": "I would define it as the use of scientific terms and principles in talking about facts about which too little is known to make prediction and control possible" (Skinner, 1984, p. 578). He emphasizes that interpretation is neither science nor philosophy but "something else" (p. 578). Thus, the fine point that Skinner makes is that his works mistakenly have been evaluated according to the criteria of science and philosophy. Consequently, evaluations of the works often conclude that they are neither good science nor good philosophy.

Skinner's definition of interpretation

makes clear that his renderings of human behavior are accounts derived from the basic assumptions of TEAB. His act of interpretation is consistent with one definition of what it means to interpret: *To conceive in the light of individual belief, judgment or circumstance* (Webster's 9th New Collegiate Dictionary, pp. 632-633). In this respect, Skinner's interpretations of human behavior are no different from those derived from any other individual's faith in a religious or political belief system and are equally untestable.

However, empirical evidence, not faith, is the central feature of science. In other words, "the business of science is not to interpret - which any Marxist, Freudian, structuralist, etc. can and does do, but to *explain*, and that is done through theories" (Bethlehem, 1987, p. 92). Because Skinner's writings are nonscientific interpretations, rather than scientific explanations, a complete understanding of his position could not lead to its widespread adoption as the science of human behavior.

Because, by his own admission, Skinner's major works are not scientific, classifying him as a great scientist is a category mistake. Instead, he more appropriately should be classified as a great interpreter on the level with Sigmund Freud. That is, Skinnerian behavior-analysis, as an interpretive system, bears a remarkable affinity to Freudian psychoanalysis. Freud developed a system to interpret the dynamics of the psyche from his observations of a few Viennese individuals. Similarly, Skinner developed a system to interpret the dynamics of human behavior from his observations of a few rats and pigeons.

Each of these interpretive systems provides post hoc, "in principle" accounts of human behavior that are based on events in the organism's past history. However, whereas psychoanalysis is not regarded by many people as being a sound, *scientific* system (e.g., Hines, 1988), behavior analysis is. Given the relative lack of scientific evidence for behavior-analytic accounts of human behavior, the scientific esteem accorded behavior analysis should be no greater than that accorded psychoanalysis. (See H. J. Eysenck, 1984, for additional discussion of the similarity between the Freudian and Skinnerian systems.)

Skinner's interpretations pose a far greater danger than just being misunderstood by adherents and critics, alike. Those who believe in the virtue of Skinner's interpretations of human behavior zealously and dogmatically advocate their incorporation into many cultural practices (e.g., Johnston & Shook, 1987; Pennypacker, 1986). Sir Karl Popper, the noted philosopher of science, recognized this danger and refused to sign the Secular Humanist Declaration II because Skinner had done so. The primary reason given by Popper for his action was that *Walden Two* and *Beyond Freedom and Dignity* are...

> worse and more dangerous than the most fundamentalist religious tract: there is a mixture of naivete, sheer ignorance, arrogation of omniscience, and Caesarian megalomania in these books, which is, in my opinion, far more urgent to combat than the churches. (Popper, 1981, p. 3)

From our perspective, the danger arises primarily because Skinner's controversial views regarding the determinants of human behavior and the structure of human society are promoted "in the name of science." That is, Skinner has taken his system, which has very little scientific support as a viable account of human behavior, and packaged it in such a manner as to have the system regarded by many academicians and nonacademicians alike as the pinnacle of scientific psychology. In this regard, Skinner can be considered not only a great interpreter, but also a great pseudoscientist.

7.5 SUMMARY: SKINNER'S ROLE

To address accurately the paradoxical influence of B. F. Skinner and TEAB inside and outside of scientific psychology, we have found it necessary to present a vast collection of evidence pertaining to numerous specific issues. In concluding this chapter, we provide the following synopsis that captures the salient features of Skinner's role in this paradox.

Skinner received little formal academic training in the content and practice of scientific psychology (Fraley & Vargas, 1986; Skinner, 1979). He took few courses, and his research was unsupervised. Thus, when Skinner accepted his first academic position, he admittedly "knew almost nothing about psychology" (1979, p. 46). Despite knowing little about the field of psychology, the basic tenets of his system were already set firmly into place.

Generally, *The Behavior of Organisms* (1938)

is regarded as Skinner's most significant work. Yet, in the words of one behavior analyst, the view of radical behaviorism presented in that book is "little more than an expression of faith" (Rachlin, 1987, p. 157). Because Skinner conducted minimal empirical research in the ensuing 50 years, he provided little evidence to justify the transition of the view expressed in 1938 from the realm of faith to the realm of science.

Instead, Skinner devoted most of his subsequent efforts to the promotion of TEAB and to the development of nonscientific interpretations of behavior. However, as Bethlehem (1987) notes, Skinner's use of interpretations "covers the inadequacy of his position by allowing him to evade recognition that the business of science is not to interpret...but to explain" (p. 92). Providing interpretations that are neither science nor philosophy enables Skinner to advance his views as having a scientific basis, while ignoring the scientific and philosophical arguments raised against them.

Skinner's self-description is that he knew little psychology. Moreover, Bethlehem (1987) notes that his work reflects "an incomprehension of the nature of science in its orthodox conception" (p. 91), adding that "if Skinner knows little of the philosophy of science, he understands less of political and ethical philosophy" (p. 93). Although the reinforcement framework relies on an analogy to evolution, Plotkin (1987a) emphasizes that Skinner ignores the use of the evolutionary analogy by others and that Skinner's use of the analogy has not inspired an empirical research program. Moreover, according to Plotkin (1987b), Skinner shows "no references in his own writings to suggest that he was widely read in biology" (p. 152). Thus, despite reliance on the evolutionary analogy, Skinner apparently did not have the requisite knowledge to draw an appropriate analogy. Rachlin (1987) concludes that "Skinner's radical behaviorism, taken by itself, is not a particularly elegant theory" (p. 157), and Hinson (1987) stresses that "many of his specific inquiries [within that framework] are of questionable value" (p. 205).

Given that Skinner's scientific work is "inelegant", "of questionable value", and apparently does not reflect much knowledge of science, psychology, biology, evolution, statistics, linguistics, sociology, and political science, nor of their associated philosophies, the question remains as to why his work has been discussed and debated so widely. The apparent answer is provided succinctly by Irving Maltzman:

> He's a great PR man, and the reason there is such an interest in Skinnerian approaches to so many problems is not because there have been some great profound advances in knowledge, or some clearly established successes, but because the guy's a great publicist. (Baars, 1986, p. 103)

8

THE FUTURE OF BEHAVIOR ANALYSIS

The picture that emerges from the previous chapters is that behavior analysts put a relatively great emphasis on broad, conceptual issues and relatively little emphasis on empirical data. This emphasis on conceptual matters runs counter to the importance that the scientific method places on data (e.g., Kuhn, 1962). A question that arises, then, is why do behavior analysts stress the conceptual at the expense of the empirical? The answer to this question apparently has two parts.

8.1 CONCEPTUAL AND EMPIRICAL ISSUES

The first part lies in the fact that behavior

analysts make a relatively clean distinction between conceptual and empirical issues and stress that data simply do not bear on conceptual issues (e.g., Harzem & Miles, 1978). As one example, Harzem and Miles note that "those who assume that Chomsky and his followers are or could be in a position, on the basis of *evidence*, to 'refute Skinner's theory of language acquisition' have missed the point" (p. 53, emphasis theirs). In other words, because Skinner's interpretation of language acquisition is conceptual, rather then empirical, it cannot be refuted by data. Thus, if one accepts the logic of conceptual and empirical issues being separate, considerable effort can be devoted to resolving conceptual issues, without recourse to data.

Because the philosophical position adopted by behavior analysts does not view data as necessarily impinging on conceptual issues, many of their attempts to justify the behavior-analytic approach do not rely on experimental evidence (e.g., Harzem, 1987; Lee, 1988; Liegland, 1984; Skinner, 1983b). Instead of promoting their views through data-based, scientific arguments, behavior analysts resort to developing agenda that promote the imposition of their views, both inside and outside of academia, through legislation (e.g., Johnston & Shook, 1987; Morris, 1985). Also, practical applications are given strong weight in justifying the reinforcement framework, rather than being seen as a stage within the scientific endeavor (e.g., Pennypacker, 1986). Given that psychology is an experimental science, psychologists will be convinced of the usefulness of a framework only by scientific data and not by legislation. Moreover, although application is desirable, it cannot by itself be taken to justify the basic theory on which the application was based.

8.2 THE SURVIVAL GOAL

At this point, it should be clear to the reader that the evidence is sufficiently great so as to warrant acceptance of the hypothesis that the basic goal of TEAB is its survival. Moreover, specification of this goal provides a salient feature around which to organize and make sense out of the positions and activities taken by many behavior analysts. For example, the relatively clean distinction between conceptual and empirical analyses (e.g., Harzem & Miles, 1978; Lee, 1988) arises because conceptual analyses involve the philosophy associated with behavior analysis (radical behaviorism), whereas empirical analyses must operate in accord with the philosophy of science (Machan, 1974). Thus, each of these analyses is governed by a different set of philosophical suppositions.

Because the survival goal of TEAB is intertwined with the philosophy associated with behavior analysis, greater importance is placed on conceptual analyses. The hypothetico-deductive reasoning that is characteristic of empirical analysis in science simply is dismissed by behavior analysts as "quasi-behavioral" (Johnston & Pennypacker, 1986). Thus, whereas most approaches operate within the mandates of the philosophy of science first, behavior analysis operates within the philosophy associated with the behavior-analytic version of behaviorism. This approach, in which behavior-analytic philosophy is given precedence, ensures that the actions of behavior analysts will remain consistent with the assumption that they engage in *the* science of behavior.

The dynamic relation of these different operating mandates to the activities of scientific psychologists and behavior analysts is depicted in Figure 8-1. Each of the respective systems emerges from the

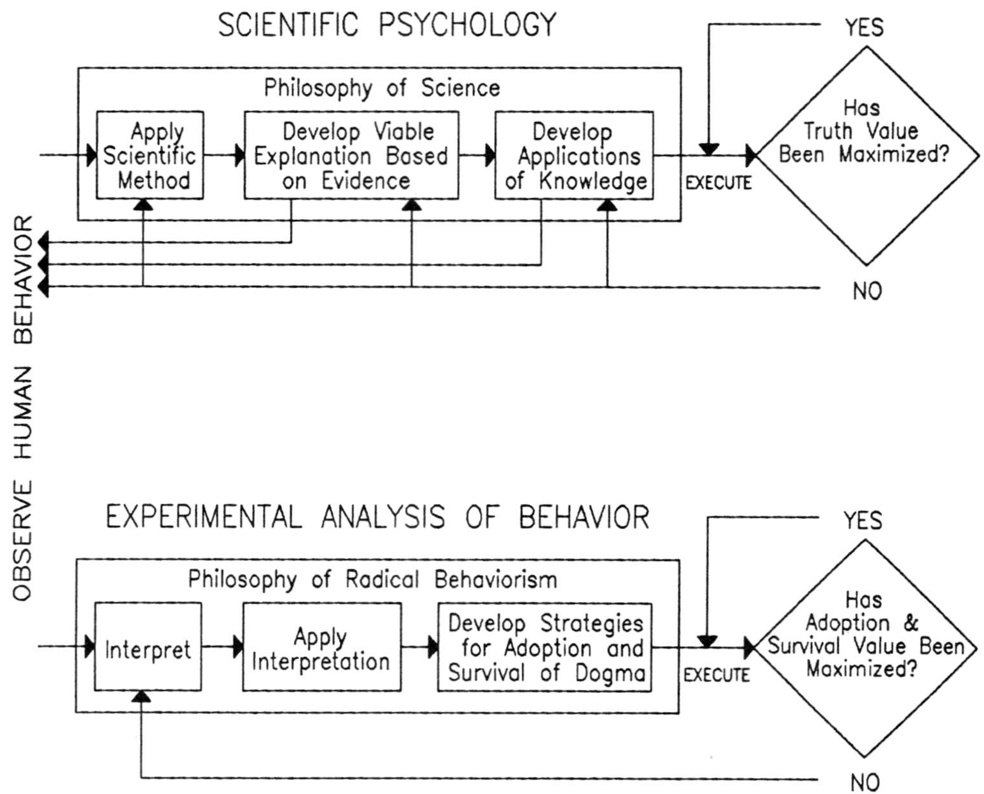

Figure 8-1. System models of operations within scientific psychology and behavior analysis.

evidence that we have presented in this book and captures many of the characteristics of the respective groups. Although the systems both begin by observing behavior and are very similar in terms of their surface structure, they differ in at least three crucial respects. First, the operating environments that are created by the separate philosophical mandates foster quite different processes that, in turn, lead to the execution of different actions. Second, the distinct goals adopted by scientific psychology and TEAB set up different criteria for evaluating the effectiveness of the actions. Third, the feedback loops in the scientific system perpetuate empiricism by leading continually to new observations derived from the science. In contrast, the feedback loops in the behavior-analytic system lead either to perseveration or to reinterpretation, which perpetuates dogma. Because the actions of the behavior-analytic system are not directed toward the goal of truth value, the importance of empirical evidence is diminished.

If behavior analysts were to lend greater weight to empirical tests of hypotheses to confirm or disconfirm behavior-analytic interpretations, the complete generality of their world view would be placed in jeopardy.

Similarly, the use of nonscientific interpretations of human behavior can be developed on the basis of the philosophy associated with the behavior-analytic approach, and as such are not required to meet the criteria dictated by the philosophy of science. Thus, again, it is not surprising that many of the actions that behavior analysts undertake in promoting these interpretations "in the name of science" seem pseudoscientific. The actions do not arise from processes cast by the philosophy of science and were not guided by the goal criterion of truth value.

The realization that the overriding goal of behavior analysis is its own survival as a distinct discipline, rather than the acquisition of scientific knowledge, also serves to clarify the restrictive definition given to science by behavior analysts. As noted earlier, the typical behavior-analytic definition of science excludes "understanding". That is, "the primary purposes of science from a behavior-analytic viewpoint [are] - prediction and control" (Hayes & Brownstein, 1986, p. 175). The key aspect of this restrictive definition of science is that it stems from "a behavior-analytic viewpoint". In other words, instead of the behavior-analytic conception of science being developed from the philosophy of science, it too has been developed with respect to the philosophy associated with behavior analysis.

If understanding were to be included in the behavior-analytic definition of science, as is done in approaches that receive their mandates from the philosophy of science, the survival of TEAB would be less assured. Inclusion of understanding would require that other alternatives be given consideration in determining the truth. Empirical evidence might then favor alternatives and rule against the behavior-analytic view. However, retaining prediction and control, while eliminating understanding, has enabled behavior analysts to maintain a veil of science in front of their primary goal of the survival of TEAB.

Given the realization that has emerged regarding the primary goal of behavior analysis, the question of the future of TEAB can be considered in two different ways. First, can the goal of survival be met by the tactics that currently are advocated? Second, if so, will that survival allow for TEAB to make systematic contributions to psychology?

8.3 A MODEL FOR SURVIVAL

The answer to the first question stated above is "yes". This answer is reflected in the systems model for TEAB by the fact that the behavior of the system is directed toward maximizing adoption and survival value. As a consequence, behavior analysts have gone to great lengths to develop survival strategies. In their book, *Strategies and Tactics of Human Behavioral Research*, Johnston and Pennypacker (1980) advocate that behavior analysts attempt to influence public and academic policy, as one tactic for ensuring survival. This tactic involves very detailed lobbying efforts intended to result in the legislated adoption of behavior analysis. Behavior-analytic efforts in these areas have been impressive.

Recently, Johnston and Shook (1987) published a historical review of the tactics and strategies that were employed to gain control of developmental services in the state of Florida. The broader intent of their review was to provide a contingency control model that could be used inside and outside of academia to further behavior-analytic interests. The range and scope of the contingencies that are manipulated as part of the model would seem to ensure a high likelihood for survival of TEAB.

According to Johnston and Shook (1987), the seminal event in the takeover of Florida's developmental services was an incident at a state institution that required outside investigation. Shortly thereafter, the director of the Division of Retardation formed a Joint Task Force. Because the incident that led to formation of the task force involved behavioral programming, behavior-analytic "experts" were well-represented. Johnston and Shook state:

> The composition of the group (containing mostly behavioral experts and yet somewhat balanced with retardation and legal experts), the highly public context of its origins, and the explicit nature of its responsibility all give its final report considerable influence, and this influence was on behalf of increasing and improving the role of behavioral programming in the state's retardation system....By establishing the general philosophy and methods of behavior analysis as the sole model for changing the behavior of retarded citizens under

> state care, it gave the field the imprimature of the state in this one area of service....Put another way, the report and its accumulating consequences formalized the state's need for the field of behavior analysis, and it did so in very specific ways that left relatively little room for bureaucratic maneuvering or attempts to substitute other models. (p. 201)

In short, behavior analysts used a public trust to ensure the singular commitment to behavior analysis within the state system. Thus, in terms of survival of TEAB, the actions had value. However, in terms of ensuring the right to effective treatment, the actions clearly are of questionable value.

After legislating behavior analysis as "the model for the treatment of retardation", a collection of restrictions was instituted that would maintain the authority of behavior analysts to implement the operation of the state system. A regulatory manual for the implementation of behavioral procedures was devised, behavior-analytic certification programs were set up, and behavior-analytic review committees were formed.

The certification program for behavior analysts has particular survival value. Through legislation, the need for qualified behavior analysts was created. Through certification, the definition of "qualified" was established. By making certification attainable only by persons who received training in behavior analysis, a demand for formal behavior-analytic training was created. Thus, the educational system now must commit "to hire more faculty with behavior analysis credentials so as to meet this increasing demand....This effect will be gradual, each new college or university faculty member that comes into the state gradually develops a range of influences on and off the campus that bode well for the discipline" (Johnston & Shook, 1987, p. 215).

Increasing the number of behavior analysts in the retardation system has cascading effects.

> It increases the likelihood that people with behavioral training will earn positions of influence in state and private settings, which then may further accelerate the influence of the discipline....Another benefit of increasing the

> number of people in the state with even the modest level of behavioral training that the certification program formally demands is that it increases the number of people who identify with behavior analysis as a discipline. (Johnston & Shook, 1987, p. 215)

To summarize, behavior analysts took advantage of a fortuitous opportunity to build an ecosystem in which a demand for behavior analysts was legislated, thus dictating that a supply be produced. However, whereas the survival goal of TEAB was served, needs of the individuals depending on these services were not served, unless TEAB is indeed *the* science of behavior.

A similar fortuitous opportunity enabled the imposition of the behavior-analytic approach on a much grander scale. Voneche (1987) relates the circumstances surrounding the adoption of behavior analysis by the Brazilian educational system.

> ...I witnessed it myself in Brazil, when the regime switched from the left to the right through a military *putsch* the Faculty of the

> National University of Brazilia was demoted and the United States of America sent in American experts with fifty-seven Skinner boxes for teaching 'real psychology'. There was some irony in this gift to a country where thousands of people were going to be sent to jails without any lever to depress but a lot to depress about. (p. 72)

To this day, the behavior-analytic approach continues to have considerable influence in the educational systems of Central and South America (see, e.g., Keller, 1986).

More generally, Johnston and Shook (1987) describe the success of the Florida Association for Behavior Analysis and note a number of key features in its success. According to them, two characteristics are crucial: (1) "that the association has its base in the area of retardation" and (2) "that its primary membership focus is on individuals who have less than graduate-level training in behavior analysis" (p. 217). The first of these characteristics brings "immediate visibility and legitimacy to the professional group" (p. 218). The second characteristic "has the advantage of numbers....[and thus] gives an organization far greater potential for financial survival" (p. 218).

After describing the Florida system, Johnston and Shook (1987) propose general principles for state-level development. These principles are: (1) establish a paraprofessional focus; (2) base effort in human services system; (3) establish broad and coordinated efforts of academics; (4) organize a state professional association; and (5) develop training contingencies.

The general principles that Johnston and Shook (1987) extrapolated from the Florida system seem appropriate to the task of ensuring the survival of TEAB. In fact, Johnston and Shook point out that such state-level development can make an important contribution to meeting the national goals of the behavior-analytic agenda. These are "the national goal[s] of increasing the number of behavior analysts on university and college faculty....[and] to influence public policy in ways consistent with behavioral philosophy and literature" (p. 231). In short, if these goals are met, the survival of TEAB as a distinct discipline seems likely.

8.4 CONTRIBUTIONS TO PSYCHOLOGY

Given that the agenda of TEAB is well suited to its survival, the next question is whether systematic contributions to psychology will be a by-product. The answer seems to be "no", because the actions of TEAB are guided by the overriding goal of the survival of TEAB rather than by the goal of scientific truth-value. This is not to say that periodic contributions are impossible, only that they will be relatively infrequent and unsystematic. By allowing their survival goal to be dictated solely by behavior-analytic philosophy, the activities in which behavior analysts engage in pursuit of that goal often are in conflict with the goals of science. Thus, the only way to ensure the survival of TEAB is for behavior analysts not to engage in the science of psychology, which means that they will continue to have little impact. To make systematic contributions to psychology, behavior analysts would have to open up to scrutinization vis-a-vis the scientific method. However, to do so requires recognition of understanding and truth-value as components of science and places the future of TEAB as a distinct discipline in jeopardy.

Previously, we proposed that for behavior

analysts to have the potential for contributing further to psychology, they must redefine their primary goal from that of survival as a distinct discipline to that of "seeking the truth, wherever it may lie" (Proctor & Weeks, 1988, p. 139). In short, to contribute to psychology, behavior analysts will have to make a fundamental change in the primary goal that currently guides their actions. Such a change requires that radical behaviorism not be accepted as a world view but only as one approach to be evaluated relative to competing approaches.

One example of an appropriately-directed effort involves a collaborative project that has resulted in a procedure for teaching breast self-examination as an aid to the early detection of cancer (Pennypacker, 1986). The procedure was derived from a psychophysical and behavioral analysis of detecting small tumors in a facsimile of the human breast. The primary research was published in the journals *Perception & Psychophysics* (Adams, Hall, Pennypacker, Goldstein, Hench, Madden, Stein, & Catania, 1976; Bloom, Criswell, Pennypacker, Catania, & Adams, 1982), *Cancer* (Hall, Stephenson, Adams, Goldstein, Pennypacker, & Stein, 1980; Saunders, Pilgrim, & Pennypacker, 1986), and *Journal of Biomedical Engineering* (Madden,

Hench, Hall, Adams, Goldstein, Pennypacker, & Stein, 1978).

In his presidential address to the Association for Behavior Analysis, Pennypacker (1986) used this research and the resulting technology as an example for behavior analysts to follow. He characterized it as an example of the development of "behavioral technology" and advocated marketing of such technologies, because "if behavior analysis is to survive, *its* technologies must survive" (p. 149, emphasis ours). But this technology does not belong to behavior analysis. Rather, unimpeded by behavior-analytic philosophy, the hybrid technology developed as a result of collaborative efforts. Thus, ironically, instead of lauding the benefits of the eclectic approach taken in that project, Pennypacker claimed the project as yet another triumph for behavior analysis.

The primary emphasis of Pennypacker's (1986) address was on the importance of promoting public consumption of behavior-analytic technologies. To this end, he summarized the strategies and tactics that were employed in the marketing of the breast self-examination procedure. These strategies and tactics involved an analysis of the contingencies of the market place. By

Pennypacker's assessment, the success in marketing the procedure has been impressive. The strategies and tactics used in the marketing were similar to those described by Johnston and Shook (1987). Given that these latter authors developed a contingency-based model for the survival of behavior analysis, more generally, we are not surprised that similar procedures meet with success in a more limited situation. Again, the marketing of the breast examination procedure is a good example of the resourcefulness of behavior analysts at using various means to maximize the adoption and survival of TEAB.

The basic empirical foundation for this application resides in contemporary, mainstream experimental psychology. That a useful technology could be developed from such a source is not surprising to us. What is surprising is that behavior analysts would be willing to make use of this knowledge from contemporary psychology, while at the same time collectively disregarding and disparaging the remaining literature as "unscientific".

It should be clear from the breast self-examination example that if behavior analysts were to familiarize themselves with the vast literature of contemporary psychology, they likely would find that much of that literature is of value in providing opportunities for productive interactions. However, until truth-value takes precedence over survival-value, such interactions will be infrequent, and the resulting contributions to psychology will be minimal.

Another possible avenue for behavior analysts to take that could lead to renewed participation in the science of human behavior is suggested by Harzem and Miles' (1978) conceptual analysis of TEAB. In concluding their analysis, Harzem and Miles note that "it is likely...that certain stimuli can control responding *even though they were not previously associated with reinforcement* (p. 124, emphasis theirs). They propose that such stimuli be called "*informative stimuli,* since they appear to have their effect on behavior by providing information" (p. 124).

Harzem and Miles then stress the crucial point that an explanation of human behavior in terms of reinforcement history is problematic because it "is a *post hoc* explanation; and it has the disadvantage of discouraging further research by suggesting that an account of the phenomenon is already available" (p. 125). They go on to note that "in contrast, the concept of an *informative stimulus* raises questions for experiment" (p.

125).

Harzem and Miles (1978) seem to be unaware that through their conceptual analysis they have struck on the primary reason, dictated long ago by the empirical evidence, for the rise of cognitive psychology. That is, the notion that stimuli provide information that must then be acted on is at the heart of the information-processing framework that underlies much research in cognitive psychology, as well as of other productive frameworks that have been used to study such topics as perception (e.g., Gibson, 1979) and Pavlovian conditioning (e.g., Davey, 1987; Rescorla, 1988). Thus, one reason why the volume of behavioral research on humans from the behavior-analytic perspective is but a small fraction of the research generated by other perspectives is that the other perspectives lead to more and better research questions.

That behavior analysts show some concern that the informational properties of stimuli may be important suggests a point of entry for TEAB into contemporary, scientific psychology. Through exploring the roles and relations between the reinforcing and informational aspects of stimuli, behavior analysts potentially could make valuable contributions to contemporary psychology.

However, such contributions will not come easily, because the literature with which behavior analysts must become familiar is voluminous, interdisciplinary, and relatively advanced and formalized. Thus, the existence of TEAB as a viable member of the scientific community depends on the ability of its adherents to master the knowledge of contemporary psychology and to show that an integration of behavior-analytic concepts into that knowledge provides additional insight. Consequently, behavior analysts must abandon the grandiose survival strategy of *becoming* psychology and adopt the more scientifically valid strategy of *contributing* to psychological knowledge.

9

THE FUTURE OF PSYCHOLOGY

Our analysis of the specific relation between TEAB and psychology has highlighted the more general problem of coexistence of scientific approaches that develop different goal structures. Any field of inquiry that attempts to obtain scientific status without placing truth-value as its highest goal creates an environment that is counterproductive to obtaining systematic, scientific knowledge. Contemporary psychology is characterized by generally unified efforts at uncovering the psychological principles of behavior. However, in recent years there has been a tendency for different primary goals to be developed for the science and practice of psychology.

In this final chapter, we examine implications of our analysis of the goal structure of TEAB for the future of psychology. Specifically, two points are addressed. First, we consider the general consequences for the field of psychology that could result from a division of primary goals. Second, we consider the way in which the niche created by this division sets the occasion for the opportunistic survival strategies of TEAB to flourish at the expense of truth-value.

9.1 A POLARIZATION OF PROFESSIONAL CONCERNS

Despite the vitality that the field of psychology has enjoyed, it currently is disturbed by a polarization of professional concerns between basic scientists and practitioners (e.g., Fowler, 1988). The primary concern of basic scientists is the establishment of a sound body of psychological data and theory. In contrast, the primary concern of practitioners is the application of psychological knowledge to urgent problems that require immediate solutions.

As is captured by the model in Figure 8-1, both basic research and derived application are integral parts of psychological science that must be directed by common scientific concerns. If the current polarization leads to a formal split that results in a dissociation between the philosophical mandates of science and those deemed relevant to the discipline, progress toward a scientific understanding of human behavior will be impeded. As we have shown in the case of TEAB, such a dissociation can result in the formulation of misplaced goals, which can lead to a wide range of extraneous activities. The culmination is a lack of scientific communication with others and, in turn, only a minor impact on the core discipline.

Despite the fact that the discipline of psychology currently is disturbed by the polarization of professional concerns, scientists and practitioners enjoy a mutual interest in examining and understanding the psychological bases of behavior. Not only do the scientists and practitioners have this mutual interest, but they also have set in place a common base of concepts and terms that provide a language for communication. In contrast, TEAB has developed a unique outlook on behavior, with an accompanying "verbal repertoire" that is distinct from that of psychology and, thus, affords little opportunity for communication.

Even though various psychologists differ in their philosophical approaches to psychology and in their specific interests, virtually all share a common adherence to the philosophy of science. For example, as discussed in previous chapters, although humanistic psychologists, psychotherapists and cognitive psychologists adopt quite different philosophies in their approaches to the study of human behavior, they share a common bond in their allegiance to the philosophy of science. It is the relative stability afforded by the scientific method that enables the truth value of alternative approaches to be evaluated. It also ensures that applications will not stand completely at odds with the scientific foundation that supports them.

The importance of placing the philosophy of the particular approach subservient to the philosophy of science is that it sets the stage for the operation of a closed-loop system in the pursuit of knowledge. That is, the logic associated with the philosophy of one's particular approach can be checked against the referent of correctness provided by evidence gathered through application of the scientific method (see Figure 8-1). Thus, in this manner, empirical data can provide guidance, with evidence either for or against a particular approach. The loop is closed, because an error-correcting mechanism is built in to determine whether a particular approach, or an alternative, is feasible.

In contrast, when the philosophical mandates of a particular approach are allowed to dictate the manner in which knowledge is pursued, the stage is set for a primarily open-loop system. That is, empirical evidence no longer can serve a guidance function, because it is not collected or evaluated via the impartial mandates of the scientific method. Thus, rather than providing empirical evidence regarding the value of the approach for understanding behavioral phenomena, only empirical demonstrations consistent with the interpretations provided by the philosophical approach can be generated.

In other words, the closed-loop process of science, by way of its error-correcting mechanism, assures that your approach will never be too deviant; the open-loop process driven by the philosophical concerns of the particular approach does not provide a similar assurance. In the case of TEAB, it is interesting that the only feedback loop for changing the actions of the system is in reference to adoption and survival value (see

Figure 8-1).

Although psychology typically has operated within the closed-loop mode engendered by adhering to the philosophy of science, the current polarization of scientists and practitioners threatens to break the loop. When decisions of practical importance are made on the basis of the interests and needs of particular groups, rather than on the basis of scientific concerns, the guiding function of scientific evidence is diminished. This sets up the potential for a lack of communication to develop between those who are interested more in practical concerns and those who are interested more in the basic science.

The polarization within psychology seems to reflect just such a lack of communication. Scientists contribute to this lack of communication by often failing (a) to be familiar with the problems faced by practitioners and (b) to deliver pertinent findings to the practitioners in a usable form. By the same token, practitioners frequently are impatient and fail to consider the pain-staking attention to detail in scientific research that is required to establish the validity and generality of a theoretical application. If the split between scientists and practitioners is allowed to become complete, each group will develop separate goals, rather than the common goal of science.

By severing the ties, practitioners likely will become less disposed toward maintaining a scientific attitude and less aware of scientific advances. Thus, an environment will be created in which pseudoscientific applications can flourish. Similarly, scientists likely will suffer from such a split, becoming increasingly esoteric in their activities. Thus, to avoid these undesirable consequences, both scientists and practitioners must work together to maintain the common goal of science and the importance of truth-value in its pursuit.

To alleviate the disturbance brought about by the polarization between concerns of science and practice, both parties must seek to reaffirm their common goal and mutual commitment to the philosophy of science. Scientists must become more informed about the problems facing the practitioners and promote ways in which the basic knowledge of psychology can be applied more effectively. Similarly, practitioners must recognize that the scientific method is constrained to proceed in an inherently conservative manner, with extensions of basic knowledge to applied problems being made judiciously.

9.2 DEPOLARIZATION OF PROFESSIONAL CONCERNS

One likely means for depolarizing professional concerns of scientists and practitioners and reaffirming their common goal would be the adoption of a model for training graduate students that is sympathetic to the needs of both groups. Such a premise underlies the Boulder model of clinical training that was proposed in 1949 (Raimy, 1950) and that has since been the dominant model for such training (Bickman, 1987). The Boulder model provides that the professional psychologist be trained as both a scientist and a practitioner (Bickman, 1987). The success of the Boulder model has been limited (Spence, 1987), but the basic premise of the model is sound.

Typically, the limited success of the Boulder model is attributed to an inability of many clinical practitioners also to be trained fully as scientists (e.g., Spence, 1987). However, we see the failings of the model as being due to (a) an improper goal and (b) its narrow application. The improper goal is that practitioners also be fully trained to be scientific researchers. This goal is unrealistic because "there are very few individuals who have the talent, the inclination, the flexibility, or the time to take on the demands of both of these roles" (Spence, 1987, p. 1052). A more realistic goal would be for all practitioners to receive a thorough background in scientific psychology that is sufficient for them to maintain a scientific attitude and be prudent consumers, i.e., to be able to understand, critically evaluate, and apply the contributions of basic psychological research.

The second failing, that of narrow application, involves the restriction of the Boulder model to clinical training. A consequence of this restriction is that training programs for basic researchers typically do not require much exposure of graduate students to the practice of psychology. For a scientist/practitioner training model to be successful at reducing the polarization of professional concerns, it must be broadly instituted.

Because being fully trained as both a scientist and a practitioner is an unrealistic goal for most individuals, the model that we advocate is one in which the relative weights afforded each of the two components will vary as a function of the individual's primary interest. In other words, the practitioner should be trained with a "practitioner/scientist" emphasis, whereas the scientist should be trained with a "scientist/practitioner" emphasis. Put simply, regardless of the individual's specific philosophical approach, one goal of training should be to make all students functionally literate in both the science and practice of psychology. The adoption of such a weighted training model by the discipline of psychology could go a long way toward eliminating the division between scientists and practitioners and, hence, make psychology a stronger, more unified scientific discipline.

The current polarization within psychology is widely acknowledged and receives lively debate in many forums. Thus, it is unlikely that a formal, complete split between scientists and practitioners could go unnoticed. However, it is much more likely that subtle shifts in goals and overriding philosophical directives could go unnoticed. As should be evident from the preceding chapters, separate goals can have grave consequences for the advancement of scientific knowledge.

One consequence of disparate goals for scientists and practitioners would be to allow for the incursion of practices that do not have the primary goal of advancing scientific knowledge regarding behavior.

Rather, these practices would be involved more with the advocacy of particular philosophical positions and tactics that ensure the longevity of particular approaches. Moreover, the subtle nature of these practices would enable events to take place under the veil of science and thus afford them considerable legitimacy and respectability.

9.3 LEGITIMACY AND RESPECTABILITY OF TEAB

Despite their frequent claims to the contrary (e.g., Epstein, 1984; Fraley & Vargas, 1986; Skinner, 1987), we have found that the scientific legitimacy and respectability accorded B. F. Skinner and TEAB far outweigh the evidence in support of their cause. As we already have documented, the public's perception is that Skinner is the premier scientific psychologist. Within academia, he generally is regarded as an oracle with respect to behavioral science and psychology.

An example of the respectability accorded Skinner as a scientist is that he serves as a fellow of the Committee for the Scientific Investigation of Claims of the Paranormal. That committee is intended to represent the voice of reason from scholars that oppose nonscientific dogma, and its official journal, the *Skeptical Inquirer*, is devoted to debunking pseudoscientific claims. Thus, the strange situation exists in which a person who has veiled dogma with science is on a committee that is dedicated to unveiling dogma. As a consequence, we doubt that the committee can progress beyond debunking Big Foot, Shirley MacLaine, the Loch Ness monster, and the like, to addressing more realistic threats to the progress of science.

Even within behavioral science, excessive scientific legitimacy and respectability are accorded Skinner and behavior analysis. For example, the *Behavioral and Brain Sciences* (*BBS*), which is an interdisciplinary forum for the discussion of issues of broad importance to the behavioral sciences, has an associate editor, A. Charles Catania, specifically for behavior analysis. Given the relatively low profile that behavior analysis enjoys within psychology and the small percentage of behavioral researchers who identify with that approach, it is impressive that the *BBS* would deem it necessary to have an associate editor devoted exclusively to TEAB.

However, a consequence of having an associate editor for an area defined so narrowly as TEAB is evident in a recent issue of the *BBS*. In that issue, several of Skinner's earlier works were reprinted, along with commentary, under the title, *The canonical papers of B. F. Skinner* (Catania, 1984). These works subsequently have been published yet again in the form of a book (Catania & Harnad, 1988). The events that set the stage for the republication of Skinner's works in a prestigious journal devoted to behavior science are related by Catania, who instigated their republication. According to Catania, when he was appointed to the editorial board in 1980, "My task was to invite or encourage authors [in the area of TEAB] to submit works that would eventually become '*BBS*' treatments" (Catania, 1988, p. xiii). Yet, he notes that "after the first couple of years of my *BBS* term I had been singularly unsuccessful in generating new material....Not one of the authors I had suggested had yet come through with a manuscript" (p. xiii).

To fill this void, Catania, who is a former student of Skinner's, and Stevan Harnad, the journal's editor, made an editorial decision to republish Skinner's works. Thus, these works, which Skinner characterizes as nonscientific and nonphilosophical interpretations, were reprinted and showcased in a journal dedicated to science. This "canonization" of Skinner's works occurred primarily because the associate editor had been unable to generate any new papers on behavior analysis that were suitable for *BBS* treatment.

Finally, within psychology, Skinner has been allowed to air his unsubstantiated opinions regularly in the *American Psychologist*, the professional voice of the American Psychological Association. These opinions have denigrated various approaches within psychology, disparaged the state of contemporary psychology, and advocated behavior analysis as *the* approach to the study of human behavior. Thus, at all levels, Skinner, in particular, and TEAB, in general, have been accorded far more credibility than they have earned on the basis of their contributions to science.

Given that the current polarization within psychology places the discipline in a fragile state, the potential for harm from those whose goals are inconsistent with those of the psychological sciences is great. As we have shown, TEAB does have a different goal structure that fosters justification of nonscientific means for the adoption and survival of their practices. Thus, if the current polarization is allowed to continue, the stage will be set for the widespread adoption of practices that are veiled deceptively in science.

9.4 ON DECEPTION

That deception is an allowable means by which to promulgate the survival goal of TEAB has precedence in the behavior-analytic literature. An advocacy of deception regarding the nature and intent of behavior analysis was depicted in *Walden Two* (Skinner, 1948). In that novel, concern about the relation of Walden Two to the larger community leads the Manager of Public Relations to provide the community with "anticipatory propaganda" regarding the practice of religion. That is, in the fictional community of Walden Two, the conception of humans is not taken from theology and no religious training is given. However, the public is misled in this regard, as described by Frazier, a central character in the novel:

> Our services are sometimes misrepresented. Our Public Relations man insists that we invite each clergyman in the neighboring towns to late Sunday

> dinner, with his family, perhaps once a year. We feed them well, and they always accept readily. They usually attend one of our services. We read from the Bible that day, since they all seem to regard Confucious as a heathen, and our chorus sticks to Bach or Handel. I call it deception, but I've been overruled. The argument is that we're fighting bigotry, and must meet it on its own terms. (p. 200)

Consistent with the fictional scenario described in *Walden Two*, misrepresentation of TEAB to the public is advocated by Baer, who recommends that behavior analysts "develop non behavior-analytic talk for public display" (Baer et al., 1987, p. 316) and try "not talking like a behavior analyst to people who think that they have free will" (Baer, 1987, p. 336).

Deception is advocated not only when dealing with the public, but also when interacting with other psychologists and academicians. For example, although behavior analysts oppose a hypothetico-deductive research strategy (e.g., Johnston & Pennypacker, 1980), Keller (1987) muses about how John Boren, the second editor of the *Journal of the Experimental Analysis of Behavior*, "introduced a test of theory into his doctoral dissertation in order to make it more appealing to examiners who liked hypotheses and their confirmation" (p. 454).

Baer et al. (1987) advocate similar deception of academicians in a recent article in which they note that self-reports and participant-observers' ratings "would not often seem to have applied significance" (p. 317) for behavior analysts. Yet, they recommend inclusion of such measures in grant proposals, because "within the small world of professional ritual, it is worth noting that the use of such measures...has a certain social validity...[and] increases the probability of the proposal being approved and funded when the proposal's reviewers are not behavior-analytic (which is almost always)" (p. 317). Baer et al. note that any resulting criticism of the proposal "at least...will be criticism within the context of approval for playing the correct game" (p. 317). Although Baer et al. seem to view the ad hoc inclusion of rating measures that are regarded as useless as "fighting bigotry...on its own terms" (Skinner, 1948, p. 200), it is deception.

Deception also is used by behavior analysts

to enhance the prestige of their field. Kay Dinsmoor (1987), the Business Manager of the *Journal of the Experimental Analysis of Behavior* since its inception, notes that the journal uses the Psychology Department at Indiana University as a mailing address, despite the fact that the department provides neither space nor staff. In her words, "*JEAB* [the *Journal of the Experimental Analysis of Behavior*] benefits from having its name associated with a university and a department well known for its excellence in research" (p. 473).

Within the field, deception also is used to misrepresent the esteem accorded individual behavior analysts. In most learned societies, an invited address is an honor that is bestowed only on prominent individuals and, thus, carries considerable prestige within the academic community. However, up through the 1988 convention of the Association for Behavior Analysis, the criterion for invited addresses was only that the individual had presented a paper at a previous meeting of the association. In other words, subsequent to a person's first presented paper, he/she was put on the association's current list of Invited Presenters and "invited" each year to present a paper at the annual convention.

The consequence of the policy for invited addresses was that such addresses were much more numerous than uninvited ones, approaching an asymptote for which "the number of invited presenters will eventually equal the membership" (Chamberlain, 1988, p. 11). An additional consequence is apparent when one considers that at the 1987 meeting of the Association for Behavior Analysis in Nashville, attendees were treated to a presentation by Tom T. Hall, the country-music entertainer. Following the above criterion, Mr. Hall would now be among the list of invited presenters.

The initial purpose for "honoring" so many individuals with invited presentations apparently was to aid presenters in getting travel money for the convention from their employers. It is easier to get money for a "prestigious" invited address than for an uninvited one. Fortunately, this dubious procedure was altered for the 1989 convention, with the term "address" being used in place of the former terms "paper" and "invited address" and a small number of invited presentations being solicited on the basis of the individual's merit (Chamberlain, 1988).

The decision to legitimize the honor of an invited address at the convention was long overdue. However, the impetus for this change was not entirely concern with the deceptive nature of the previous practice, but rather with "the cost of sending invitations and notifying the invited presenters of their convention scheduling" (p. 12). An ancillary benefit of the change, noted by Shery Chamberlain, the convention manager for 1988, is that invited presentations now will be selected "*on the basis of the individual's current research and importance to the field*" (p. 12), as should have been the case from the beginning.

9.5 FURTHER CONSEQUENCES

The deceptive practices described in the previous section and the political-action agenda that behavior analysts advocate do not make much sense when considered in isolation. However, these practices are sensible when viewed in light of the primary goal of the adoption of behavior-analytic views and the survival of TEAB as a distinct discipline. That is, virtually no activity is unwarranted if it leads to fulfillment of this survival goal, because the goal arises from the fundamental assumption that TEAB is *the* science of behavior. If the basic assumption is that your views are "true", then essentially any means are allowable for seeing that those views are adopted.

Given their basic assumption, and the goals derived from it, it is clear that the only way in which behavior analysts desire for TEAB to *become* psychology is by *replacing* psychology. In terms of survival value, this is the ultimate tactic. Thus, both scientists and practitioners should keep in mind that the primary goal that guides the actions of behavior analysts does not necessarily make TEAB sensitive to the best interests of scientific psychology.

As one example, Drash (1988) recommends that "*scientific behaviorism* be subsitituted for *radical behaviorism* as the designation for the philosophy [radical behaviorism] of the science of behavior" (p. 88). In other words, Drash's recommendation is to make the terms *scientific behaviorism* and *radical behaviorism* synonymous. Drash is clear on the rationale for his proposal:

> Since Skinner's objective was to establish a science of behavior from the beginning (Skinner, 1979, p. 342), and since *radical behaviorism* is the established formal designation of B. F.

> Skinner's philosophy of science..., Skinner's position is then naturally equated with the science of behaviorism or *scientific behaviorism*. (p. 88)

In addition to the obvious gain in respectability that would accompany this semantic juggling, Drash emphasizes that "this change allows us to designate Skinner as the father of *scientific behaviorism*" (p. 88). That a behavior analyst would propose reinterpreting history only serves to highlight that virtually any means in pursuit of the survival goal is justifiable. Thus, some behavior analysts hold the basic assumption that TEAB is *the* science of behavior with such strong conviction that a formal distortion of history is advocated.

Given the self-serving activities advocated by behavior analysts in pursuit of their survival goal, we are disturbed at the major role that they have played in representing the "scientists" in the recent establishment of the American Psychological Society. This newly founded society is intended for scientists as an alternative organization to the American Psychological Association, which exists for both scientists and practitioners. Division 25 (Experimental Analysis of

Behavior) of the American Psychological Association was the first division to support the American Psychological Society progenitor, the Assembly for Scientific and Applied Psychology. Moreover, it is the first division of the American Psychological Association to affiliate formally with the American Psychological Society (*APS Observer*, 1989, May, p. 14).

The ground-level involvement of TEAB in a society that is intended to provide a scientific alternative to the American Psychological Association is cause for concern. The concern arises from those issues that prompted us to conduct the investigations that are summarized in this book. Specifically, as a result of our first-hand observation of the dissolution of an eclectic psychology department and our subsequent investigation of the behavior-analytic literature, we were led to discover that the behavior-analytic position precludes an eclectic approach to the science of psychology.

One of the most prominent themes of the behavior-analytic literature is that TEAB and psychology cannot share the same discipline. In light of the strong statements to this effect that are presented throughout this book, we are forced to question the motives behind the role played by behavior analysts in the development of the American Psychological Society. These motives are particularly important, given that the directions taken by this society will be of critical importance for the future of a unified science of psychology. Indeed, in reference to this importance, Skinner has stated, "The American Psychological Society seems to me to be the natural next step in the furtherance of psychology as a science" (Scarr, 1989).

That Skinner would support this society as the "natural" next step in the development of psychology as a science is of concern, given the incompatibility of TEAB and contemporary psychology that is so widely acknowledged, supported, and discussed by him and other behavior analysts. If the American Psychological Society is to provide a viable scientific alternative to the American Psychological Association, then it is important that the Society maintain a conception of science that is independent of a particular philosophy of behavior. Can such a conception be maintained while at the same time allowing for the promotion of the intolerant "behavior-analytic" conception, which is advocated by members such as the Society's first secretary-treasurer and

Editor of the *APS Observer*, Stephen Hayes (Hayes & Brownstein, 1986)? If there is to be co-prosperity of behavior analysts and other psychologists in any society devoted to the science of psychology, then there must be successful resolution of this important issue.

We do not advocate that persons be excluded from any organization devoted to scientific psychology on the basis of their particular approach, nor are we suggesting that the general intent behind the development of the American Psychological Society is not sincere. However, we are wary of the consequences that may arise from behavior analysts playing a major role in such an organization, since their goal is the unconditional adoption and survival of TEAB.

In this book, we have tried to enlighten psychologists to the fact that the survival goal of TEAB often is portrayed as consistent with the goals of science, but it is not. Behavior analysts promote a world view that embodies the fundamental assumption that TEAB is *the* science of behavior and that contemporary psychology is not. However, defining *a priori* the scope of activities that are allowed to constitute the science of psychology can only impede the progress of an empirical, scientific analysis of behavior.

The importance of adhering to an unprejudiced approach to science in the discipline of psychology was stated eloquently by the eminent psychologist, R. S. Woodworth, in the Columbia University Lectures of 1916-1917:

> Though attempts to define the scope of a science are not without value, they are not fundamental. A science does not take its start from a definition, as if its task were assigned to it by some higher authority, but it proceeds from problem to problem, often taking unexpected turns as the knowledge gained opens vistas of knowledge still to be sought. (Woodworth, 1918, pp. 20-21)

REFERENCES

Adams, C. K., Hall, D. C., Pennypacker, H. S., Goldstein, M. K., Hench, L. L., Madden, M. C., Stein, G. H., & Catania, A. C. (1976). Lump detection in simulated human breasts. *Perception & Psychophysics, 20*, 163-167.

Amsel, A. (1989). *Behaviorism, neobehaviorism, and cognitivism in learning theory*. Hillsdale, NJ: Lawrence Erlbaum.

Anderson, J. R. (1983). *The architecture of cognition*. Cambridge, MA: Harvard University Press.

APS Observer (1989, May).

Articles of association (1962). American Association of Humanistic Psychology.

Baars, B. J. (1986). *The cognitive revolution in psychology*. New York: Guilford.

Baer, D. M. (1987). Weak contingencies, strong contingencies, an many behaviors to change. *Journal of Applied Behavior Analysis, 20*, 335-338.

Baer, D. M., Wolf, M. M., & Risley, T. R. (1987). Some still-current dimensions of applied behavior analysis. *Journal of Applied Behavior Analysis, 20*, 313-328.

Baron, A., Kaufman, A., Stauber, K. A. (1969). Effects of instructions and reinforcement feedback on human operant behavior maintained by fixed-interval reinforcement. *Journal of the Experimental Analysis of Behavior, 12*, 701-712.

Berger, D. E., Pezdek, K., & Banks, W. P. (Eds.) (1987). *Applications of cognitive psychology: Problem solving, education, and computing*. Hillsdale, NJ: Lawrence Erlbaum.

Bethlehem, D. (1987). Scolding the carpenter. In S. Modgil & C. Modgil (Eds.), *B. F. Skinner: Consensus and controversy* (pp. 89-97). New York: Falmer Press.

Bickman, L. (1987). Graduate education in psychology. *American Psychologist, 42,* 1041-1047.

Blackman, D. (1974). *Operant conditioning: An experimental analysis of behaviour.* London: Metheun.

Bloom, H. S., Criswell, E. L., Pennypacker, H. S., Catania, A. C., & Adams, C. K. (1982). Major stimulus dimensions determining detection of simulated breast lesions. *Perception & Psychophysics, 32,* 251-260.

Blough, D. S. (1987). Counterpoint. *Journal of the Experimental Analysis of Behavior, 48,* 468-469.

Boff, K. R., Kaufman, L., & Thomas, J. P. (Eds.) (1986). *Handbook of perception and human performance* (Vols. I and II). New York: John Wiley.

Boff, K. R., & Lincoln, J. E. (Eds.) (1988). *Engineering data compendium: Human perception and performance.* Wright-Patterson Air Force Base, OH: Harry G. Armstrong Aerospace Medical Research Laboratory.

Boring, E. G. (1950). *A history of experimental psychology* (2nd Ed.). New York: Appleton-Century-Crofts.

Bower, G. H. (1975). Cognitive psychology: An introduction. In W. K. Estes (Ed.), *Handbook of learning and cognitive processes: Volume 1. Introduction to concepts and issues* (pp. 25-80). Hillsdale, NJ: Lawrence Erlbaum.

Bower, G. H., & Hilgard, E. R. (1981). *Theories of learning* (5th ed.). Englewood Cliffs, NJ: Prentice-Hall.

Brady, J. V. (1987). Back to baseline. *Journal of the Experimental Analysis of Behavior, 48*, 458-459.

Brammer, L. M., & Shostrum, E. L. (1977). *Therapeutic psychology: Fundamentals of counseling and psychotherapy*. Englewood Cliffs, NJ: Prentice-Hall.

Buie, J. (1988). Skinner: Absent but not silent. *APA Monitor, 19*, 21.

Buskist, W. F. (1983). Introduction. *The Psychological Record, 33*, 451-456.

Buskist, W. F. (1987). On talking to ourselves. *Behavior Analysis*, *22*, 1-2.

Cameron, N. (1943). The paranoid pseudocommunity. *American Journal of Sociology*, *49*, 32-38.

Capaldi, E. J., & Miller, D. J. (1988). Counting in rats: Its functional significance and the independent cognitive processes that constitute it. *Journal of Experimental Psychology: Animal Behavior Processes*, *14*, 3-17.

Card, S. K., Moran, T. P., & Newell, A. (1986). The model human processor: An engineering model of human performance. In K. R. Boff, L. Kaufman, & J. P. Thomas (Eds.), *Handbook of perception and human performance. Vol. II: Cognitive processes and performance* (pp. 45-1 - 45-35). New York: John Wiley.

Catania, A. C. (Ed.) (1984). The canonical papers of B. F. Skinner. *The Behavioral and Brain Sciences*, *7*, 473-724.

Catania, A. C. (1988). Preface. In A. C. Catania & S. Harnard (Eds.), *The selection of behavior* (pp. xiii-xvi). New York: Cambridge University Press.

Catania, A. C., & Harnad, S. (Eds.) (1988). *The selection of behavior*. New York: Cambridge University Press.

Cazeau, P. N., & Scott, Jr., S. D. (1979). *Exploring the unknown: Great mysteries reexamined*. New York: Plenum.

Chamberlain, S. (1988). The convention program: Changes for the future. *The ABA Newletter, 11*, 11-12.

Chase, P. N., & Wylie, R. G. (1985). Doctoral training in behavior analysis: Training generalized problem-solving skills. *The Behavior Analyst, 8*, 159-176.

Chomsky, N. (1959). Review of Skinner's *Verbal behavior*. *Language, 35*, 26-58.

Chomsky, N. (1967). Review of Skinner's *Verbal behavior*. In L. A. Jakobovits & M. S. Miron (Eds.), *Readings in the psychology of language* (pp. 142-171). Englewood Cliffs, NJ: Prentice-Hall.

Cohen, J. (1958). *Humanistic psychology.* New York: Collier.

Coleman, R. (1985). B. F. Skinner, 1926-1928: From literature to psychology. *The Behavior Analyst, 8*, 77-92.

Corsini, R. J. (Ed.) (1981). *Handbook of innovative psychotherapies.* New York: John Wiley.

Davey, G. (Ed.) (1987). *Cognitive processes and Pavlovian conditioning in humans.* New York: John Wiley.

Dews, P. B. (1970). *Festschrift for B. F. Skinner.* New York: Appleton-Century-Crofts.

Dews, P. B. (1987). An outsider on the inside. *Journal of the Experimental Analysis of Behavior, 48*, 456-462.

Dickinson, J. (1976). *A behavioral analysis of sport.* London: Lepus Books.

Dinsmoor, K. (1987). "Money's the cheapest thing we've got"? *Journal of the Experimental Analysis of Behavior, 48*, 472-473.

Donders, F. C. (1868/1969). On the speed of mental processes (W. G. Koster, Trans.). *Acta Psychologica, 30*, 412-431.

Drash, P. W. (1988). Radical behaviorism: A nonradical recommendation. *The Behavior Analyst, 11*, 87-89.

EAHB Programs (1983). *Experimental Analysis of Human Behavior Bulletin, 1*, 4-8.

Epstein, R. (1982). *Skinner for the classroom*. Champaign, IL: Research Press.

Epstein, R. (1984). The case for praxics. *The Behavior Analyst, 7*, 101-120.

Epstein, R. (1985). Animal cognition as the praxist views it. *Neuroscience and Biobehavioral Reviews, 9*, 623-630.

Eysenck, H. J. (1984). Skinner's blind eye. *The Behavioral and Brain Sciences, 7*, 686-687.

Eysenck, M. W. (1984). *A handbook of cognitive psychology*. Hillsdale, NJ: Lawrence Erlbaum.

Fantino, E., & Logan, C. A. (1979). *The experimental analysis of behavior: A biological perspective.* San Francisco: Freeman.

Fechner, G. (1860/1966). *Elements of psychophysics* (Vol. 1; E. G. Boring & D. H. Howes, Eds.; H. E. Adler, Trans.). New York: Holt, Rinehart, & Winston.

Ferster, C. B., & Skinner, B. F. (1957). *Schedules of reinforcement.* New York: Appleton-Century.

Fodor, J. A. (1983). *Modularity of mind.* Cambridge, MA: MIT Press.

Fowler, R. D. (1988, October). What will happen to APA? *APA Monitor, 19*, 2.

Fraley, L. E., & Vargas, E. A. (1986). Separate disciplines: The study of behavior and the study of the psyche. *The Behavior Analyst, 9*, 47-59.

Gardner, M. (1957). *Fads & fallacies: In the name of science.* New York: Dover.

Garfield, S. L., & Bergin, A. E. (Eds.) (1986). *Handbook of psychotherapy and behavior change*. New York: John Wiley.

Garner, W. R., Hake, H. W., & Eriksen, C. W. (1956). Operationism and the concept of perception. *Psychological Review, 63*, 149-159.

Gibson, J. J. (1979). *The ecological approach to visual perception*. Boston: Houghton Mifflin.

Guttman, N. (1977). On Skinner and Hull: A reminiscence and projection. *American Psychologist, 32*, 321-328.

Hall, D. C., Stephenson, H. S., Adams, C. K., Goldstein, M. K., Pennypacker, H. S., & Stein, G. H. (1980). Improved detection of human breast leasions following experimental training. *Cancer, 46*, 408-414.

Harzem, P. (1987). On the virtues of being a psychologist. *The Behavior Analyst, 10*, 175-181.

Harzem, P., & Miles, T. R. (1978). *Conceptual issues in operant psychology*. New York: John Wiley.

Harzem, P., & Williams, R. A. (1983). On searching for a science of human behavior. *Psychological Record, 33*, 565-574.

Hayes, L. J. (1988). Editorial. *Behavior Analysis, 23*, 1-2.

Hayes, S. C., & Brownstein, A. J. (1986). Mentalism, behavior-behavior relations, and a behavior-analytic view of the purposes of science. *The Behavior Analyst, 9*, 175-190.

Herrnstein, R. J. (1987). Reminisciences already? *Journal of the Experimental Analysis of Behavior, 48*, 448-453.

Hess, A. K. (Ed.) (1981). *Psychotherapy supervision: Theory, research, and practice*. New York: John Wiley.

Hilgard, E. R. (1987). *Psychology in America: A historical survey*. New York: Harcourt, Brace, Jovanovich.

Hineline, P. N., & Laties, V. G. (1987). Anniversaries in behavioral analysis. *Journal of Experimental Analysis of Behavior, 48*, 439-440.

Hines, T. (1988). *Pseudoscience and the paranormal*. Buffalo, NY: Prometheus.

Hinson, J. (1987). Hinson replies to Malone. In S. Modgil & C. Modgil (Eds.), *B. F. Skinner: Consensus and controvery* (pp. 204-206). New York: Falmer Press.

Hopkins, B. L. (1987). Comments on the future of applied behavior analysis. *Journal of Applied Behavior Analysis, 20*, 339-346.

Hostetler, A. J. (1988, April). Science: Few get in, most give up. *APA Monitor, 19*, 4.

Johnston, J. M., & Pennypacker, H. S. (1980). *Strategies and tactics of human behavioral research*. Hillsdale, NJ: Lawrence Erlbaum.

Johnston, J. M., & Pennypacker, H. S. (1986). Pure versus quasi-behavioral research. In A. Poling, W. Fuqua, & R. Ulrich (Eds.), *Research methods in applied behavior analysis: Issues and advances* (pp. 55-83). New York: Plenum.

Johnston, J. M., & Shook, G. L. (1987). Developing behavior analysis at the state level. *The Behavior Analyst, 10*, 199-233.

Kahneman, D., Slovic, P., & Tversky, A. (1982). *Judgment under uncertainity: Heuristics and biases.* New York: Cambridge University Press.

Kantowitz, B. H., Roediger, H. L., III, & Elmes, D. G. (1988). *Experimental psychology: Understanding psychological research* (3rd Ed.). St. Paul, MN: West.

Kelleher, R. T., & Morse, W. H. (1987). The Yerkes connection. *Journal of the Experimental Analysis of Behavior, 48*, 456-457.

Keller, F. S. (1986). A fire in Schermerhorn extension. *The Behavior Analyst, 9*, 139-146.

Keller, F. S. (1987). Columbia gems. *Journal of the Experimental Analysis of Behavior, 48*, 453-455.

Keller, F. S., & Schoenfeld, W. N. (1949). The psychology curriculum at Columbia College. *American Psychologist, 4*, 165-172.

Keller, F. S., & Schoenfeld, W. N. (1950). *Principles of psychology*. New York: Appleton-Century-Crofts.

Kerlinger, F. N. (1973). *Foundations of behavioral research* (2nd ed.). New York: Holt, Rinehart, and Winston.

Krantz, D. L. (1971). The separate worlds of operant and non-operant psychology. *Journal of Applied Behavior Analysis, 4*, 61-70.

Krippner, S., Achterberg, J., Bugental, J. F. T., Banathy, B., Collen, A., Jaffe, D. T., Hales, S., Kremer, J., Stigliano, A., Giorgi, A., May, R., Michael, D. N., & Salner, M. (1988). Whatever happened to scholarly discourse? A reply to B. F. Skinner. *American Psychologist, 10*, 819.

Kuhn, T. S. (1962). *The structure of scientific revolutions.* Chicago: University of Chicago Press.

Kunkel, J. H. (1987). The future of JABA: A comment. *Journal of Applied Behavior Analysis, 20*, 329-333.

Lachman, R., Lachman, J. L., & Butterfield, E. C. (1979). *Cognitive psychology and information processing.* Hillsdale, NJ: Lawrence Erlbaum.

Lamal, P. A. (1988). Radical behaviorism and selected theses concerning theory appraisal. *Psychological Record, 38*, 175-185.

Landers, S. (1988). Skinner joins aversives debate. *The APA Monitor, 19*, 22.

Laties, V. G. (1987). Society for the experimental analysis of behavior: The first thirty years (1957-1987). *Journal of the Experimental Analysis of Behavior, 48*, 495-512.

Lattal, K. A., & Harzem, P. (1984). Present trends and directions for the future. *Journal of the Experimental Analysis of Behavior*.

Lee, V. L. (1988). *Beyond behaviorism*. Hillsdale, NJ: Lawrence Erlbaum.

Lee, V. L. (1989). Comments about the isolation of behavior analysis. *The Behavior Analyst*, *12*, 85-87.

Liegland, S. (1984). Can radical behaviorism rescue psychology? *The Behavior Analyst*, *7*, 73-74.

Machan, T. R. (1974). *The pseudoscience of B. F. Skinner*. New Rochelle, NY: Arlington House.

Mackenzie, B. D. (1977). *Behaviourism and the limits of the scientific method*. Atlantic Highlands, NJ: Humanities Press.

Madden, M. C., Hench, L. L., Hall, D. C., Adams, C. K., Goldstein, P. K., Pennypacker, H. S., & Stein, G. H. (1978). Development of a model human breast with tumors for use in teaching breast examination. *Journal of Bioengineering, 2*, 427-435.

Malagodi, E. F., & Jackson, K. (1989). Behavior analysts and cultural analysis: Troubles and issues. *The Behavior Analyst, 12*, 17-33.

Malone, J. C., Jr. (1987a). Malone replies to Hinson. In S. Modgil & C. Modgil (Eds.), *B. F. Skinner: Consensus and controversy* (pp. 205-206). New York: Falmer Press.

Malone, J. C., Jr. (1987b). Skinner, the behavioral unit, and current psychology. In S. Modgil & C. Modgil (Eds.), *B. F. Skinner: Consensus and controversy* (pp. 193-203). New York: Falmer Press.

Marr, D. (1982). *Vision*. San Francisco: Freeman.

Maslow, A. H. (1966). *The psychology of science*. South Bend, IN: Gateway Editions.

Masterson, J. (1988). Interview with B. F. Skinner. *The Psychologist, 1*, 140-141.

McCain, G., & Segal, E. M. (1982). *The game of science* (4th Ed.). Monterey, CA: Brooks/Cole.

McPherson, A., Bonem, M., Green, G., & Osborne, J. G. (1984). A citation analysis of the influence on research of Skinner's *Verbal Behavior*. *The Behavior Analyst, 7*, 157-167.

Meissner, W. W. (1978). *The paranoid process*. New York: Jackson Aronson.

Miller, G. A., Galanter, E., & Pribram, K. H. (1960). *Plans and the structure of behavior*. New York: Henry Holt.

Miller, H. L., Jr. (1983). More than promissory? Reflections on the once and future exerimental analysis of human behavior. *Psychological Record, 33*, 551-564.

Miller, L. (1988). Behaviorism and the new science of cognition. *The Psychological Record, 38*, 3-18.

Morris, E. K. (1985). Public information, dissemination, and behavior analysis. *The Behavior Analyst, 8*, 95-110.

Morse, L. A., & Bruns, B. J. (1983). Nurturing behavioral repertoires within a nonsupportive environment. *The Behavior Analyst, 6*, 19-25.

Neisser, U. (1967). *Cognitive psychology*. New York: Appleton-Century-Crofts.

Norman, D. A. (Ed.) (1981). *Perspectives on cognitive science*. Hillsdale, NJ: Lawrence Erlbaum.

Patterson, C. H. (1986). *Theories of counseling and psychotherapy* (4th Ed.). New York: Harper & Row.

Pennypacker, H. S. (1986). The challenge of technology transfer: Buying in without selling out. *The Behavior Analyst, 9*, 147-156.

Plotkin, H. (1987a). Plotkin replies to Richelle. In S. Modgil & C. Modgil (Eds.), *B. F. Skinner: Consensus and controversy* (pp. 152-153). New York: Falmer Press.

Plotkin, H. (1987b). The evolutionary analogy in Skinner's writings. In S. Modgil & C. Modgil (Eds.), *B. F. Skinner: Consensus and controversy* (pp. 139-149). New York: Falmer Press.

Popper, K. (1981). Sir Karl Popper criticizes B. F. Skinner. *Free Inquiry, 1*(2), 3.

Posner, M. I. (1982). Cumulative development of attentional theory. *American Psychologist, 37*, 168-179.

Posner, M. I. (1986). Overview. In K. R. Boff, L. Kaufman, & J. P. Thomas (Eds.), *Handbook of perception and human performance, Vol II. Cognitive processes and performance* (pp. V-3 - V-10). New York: John Wiley.

Proctor, R. W., & Weeks, D. J. (1988). The virtues of scientific psychology: A reply to Harzem. *The Behavior Analyst, 11*, 131-140.

Rachlin, H. (1987). The explanatory power of Skinner's radical behaviorism. In S. Modgil & C. Modgil (Eds.), *B. F. Skinner: Consensus and controversy* (pp. 155-164). New York: Falmer Press.

Radner, D., & Radner, M. (1982). *Science and unreason*. Belmont, CA: Wadsworth.

Raimy, V. (Ed.) (1950). *Training in clinical psychology*. New York: Prentice-Hall.

Rescorla, R. A. (1988). Pavlovian conditioning: It is not what you think it is. *American Psychologist*, *43*, 151-160.

Reynolds, G. S. (1975). *A primer of operant conditioning* (Rev. Ed.). Glenview, IL: Scott, Foresman.

Richelle, M. (1987). Variation and selection: The evolutionary analogy in Skinner's theory. In S. Modgil & C. Modgil (Eds.), *B. F. Skinner: Consensus and controversy* (pp. 127-137). New York: Falmer Press.

Rogers, C. (1981). The formative tendency. In J. R. Royce & L. P. Mos (Eds.), *Humanistic psychology: Concepts and criticism* (pp. vii-x). New York: Plenum Press.

Royce, J. R., & Mos, L. P. (1981). *Humanistic psychotherapy: Concepts and criticisms* New York: Plenum Press.

Saunders, K. J., Pilgrim, C. A., & Pennypacker, H. S. (1986). Increased proficiency of search in breast self-examination. *Cancer, 58*, 2531-2557.

Scarr, S. (1989, July). Letter to the editor. *APS Observer, 2*, 18.

Schoenfeld, W. N. (1987). Reminiscences, you say? *Journal of the Experimental Analysis of Behavior, 48*, 464-468.

Schwartz, S. (1978). *Psychology of learning and behavior.* New York: Norton.

Schwartz, S., & Lacey, H. (1982). *Behaviorism, science, and human nature.* New York: Norton.

Shaffer, J. B. P. (1978). *Humanistic psychology*. Englewood Cliffs, NJ: Prentice-Hall.

Sidman, M. (1960). *Tactics of scientific research*. New York: Basic Books.

Sidman, M., Cresson, O. J., & Willson-Morris, M. (1974). Acquisition of matching to sample via mediated transfer. *Journal of the Experimental Analysis of Behavior, 22*, 261-273.

Skinner, B. F. (1938). *The behavior of organisms: An experimental analysis*. New York: Appleton-Century.

Skinner, B. F. (1948). *Walden two*. New York: Crowell-Collier-MacMillan.

Skinner, B. F. (1950). Are theories of learning necessary? *Psychological Review, 57*, 193-216.

Skinner, B. F. (1953). *Science and human behavior*. New York: Free Press.

Skinner, B. F (1956). A case study of the scientific method. *American Psychologist, 11*, 221-233.

Skinner, B. F. (1957). *Verbal behavior.* New York: Appleton-Century-Crofts.

Skinner, B. F. (1960). Pigeons in a pelican. *American Psychologist, 15,* 28-37.

Skinner, B. F. (1969). *Contingencies of reinforcement: A theoretical analysis.* New York: Appleton-Century-Crofts.

Skinner, B. F. (1971). *Beyond freedom and dignity.* New York: Knopf.

Skinner, B. F. (1973). Answers for my critics. In H. Wheeler (Ed.), *Beyond the punitive society* (pp. 256-266). San Francisco: Freeman.

Skinner, B. F. (1974). *About behaviorism.* New York: Knopf.

Skinner, B. F. (1978). *Reflections on behaviorism and society.* Englewood Cliffs, NJ: Prentice-Hall.

Skinner, B. F. (1979). *The shaping of a behaviorist.* New York: Knopf.

Skinner, B. F. (1982). An autobiography. In R. Epstein (Ed.), *Skinner for the classroom* (pp. 9-38). Champaign, IL: Research Press.

Skinner, B. F. (1983a). *A matter of consequences*. New York: Knopf.

Skinner, B. F. (1983b). Can the experimental analysis of behavior rescue psychology? *The Behavioral Analyst, 6*, 9-18.

Skinner, B. F. (1984). Coming to terms with private events. *Behavioral and Brain Sciences, 7*, 572-581.

Skinner, B. F. (1987). Whatever happened to psychology as the science of behavior? *American Psychologist, 42*, 780-786.

Spence, J. T. (1987). Centrifugal versus centripetal tendencies in psychology: Will the center hold? *American Psychologist, 42*, 1052-1054.

Stanovich, K. E. (1989). *How to think straight about psychology* (2nd ed.). Glenview, IL: Scott, Foresman.

Thagard, P. (1988). *Computational philosophy of science*. Cambridge, MA: The MIT Press.

The ABA Newsletter. (1988, Spring). *11*.

Townsend, J. T., & Ashby, F. G. (1983). *Stochastic models of elementary psychological processes*. New York: Cambridge University Press.

Voneche, J. J. (1987). An exercise in triviality: The epistemology of radical behaviorism. In S. Modgil & C. Modgil (Eds.), *B. F. Skinner: Consensus and controversy* (pp. 69-74). New York: Falmer Press.

Wasserman, E. A. (1983). Is cognitive psychology behavioral? *The Psychological Record*, *33*, 6-11.

Watson, J. B., & Rayner, R. (1920). Conditioned emotional reactions. *Journal of Experimental Psychology*, *3*, 1-14.

Webster's 9th Collegiate Dictionary. (1987). Springfield, MA: Merriam-Webster.

Wendt, G. R. (1949). The development of a psychological cult. *American Psychologist*, 4, 426.

Winokur, S. (1976). *A primer of verbal behavior: An operant view.* Englewood Cliffs, NJ: Prentice Hall.

Woodworth, R. S. (1918). *Dynamic psychology.* New York: Columbia University Press.

INDEX